New Directions for Teaching and Learning

Catherine M. Wehlburg
Edi

Where there's a Will . . . Motivation and Volition in College Teaching and Learning

Michael Theall
John M. Keller
Editors

Number 152 • Winter 2017
Jossey-Bass
San Francisco

Where there's a Will… Motivation and Volition in College Teaching and Learning
Michael Theall, John M. Keller (eds.)
New Directions for Teaching and Learning, no. 152
Editor-in-Chief: *Catherine M. Wehlburg*

NEW DIRECTIONS FOR TEACHING AND LEARNING, (Print ISSN: 0271-0633; Online ISSN: 1536-0768), is published quarterly by Wi
Subscription Services, Inc., a Wiley Company, 111 River St., Hoboken, NJ 07030-5774 USA.
Postmaster: Send all address changes to *NEW DIRECTIONS FOR TEACHING AND LEARNING*, John Wiley & Sons Inc., C/O The Sheri
Press, PO Box 465, Hanover, PA 17331 USA.

Information for subscribers
New Directions for Teaching and Learning is published in 4 issues per year. Institutional subscription prices for 2017 are:
Print & Online: US$454 (US), US$507 (Canada & Mexico), US$554 (Rest of World), €359 (Europe), £284 (UK). Prices are exc sive of tax. Asia-Pacific GST, Canadian GST/HST and European VAT will be applied at the appropriate rates. For more information current tax rates, please go to www.wileyonlinelibrary.com/tax-vat. The price includes online access to the current and all online ba files to January 1st 2013, where available. For other pricing options, including access information and terms and conditions, please v www.wileyonlinelibrary.com/access.

Delivery Terms and Legal Title
Where the subscription price includes print issues and delivery is to the recipient's address, delivery terms are **Delivered at Place (DA** the recipient is responsible for paying any import duty or taxes. Title to all issues transfers FOB our shipping point, freight prepaid. We endeavour to fulfill claims for missing or damaged copies within six months of publication, within our reasonable discretion and sub to availability.

Back issues: Single issues from current and recent volumes are available at the current single issue price from cs-journals@wiley.com

Publisher: *NEW DIRECTIONS FOR TEACHING AND LEARNING* is published by Wiley Periodicals, Inc., 350 Main St., Malden, MA 021 5020.

Journal Customer Services: For ordering information, claims and any enquiry concerning your journal subscription please go www.wileycustomerhelp.com/ask or contact your nearest office.
Americas: Email: cs-journals@wiley.com; Tel: +1 781 388 8598 or +1 800 835 6770 (toll free in the USA & Canada).
Europe, Middle East and Africa: Email: cs-journals@wiley.com; Tel: +44 (0) 1865 778315.
Asia Pacific: Email: cs-journals@wiley.com; Tel: +65 6511 8000.
Japan: For Japanese speaking support, Email: cs-japan@wiley.com.
Visit our Online Customer Help available in 7 languages at www.wileycustomerhelp.com/ask

Production Editor: Abha Mehta (email: abmehta@wiley.com).

View this journal online at wileyonlinelibrary.com/journal/tl

Printed in the USA by The Sheridan Group.

Address for Editorial Correspondence: Editor-in-chief, Catherine M. Wehlburg, *NEW DIRECTIONS FOR TEACHING AND LEARN*
Email: c.wehlburg@tcu.edu

Abstracting and Indexing Services
The Journal is indexed by Academic Search Alumni Edition (EBSCO Publishing); ERA: Educational Research Abstracts Online (T ERIC: Educational Resources Information Center (CSC); Higher Education Abstracts (Claremont Graduate University); SCO (Elsevier).

Cover design: Wiley
Cover Images: © Lava 4 images | Shutterstock

For submission instructions, subscription and all other information visit:
wileyonlinelibrary.com/journal/tl

From the Series Editor

About This Publication

Since 1980, *New Directions for Teaching and Learning* (NDTL) has brought a unique blend of theory, research, and practice to leaders in postsecondary education. NDTL sourcebooks strive not only for solid substance but also for timeliness, compactness, and accessibility.

The series has four goals: to inform readers about current and future directions in teaching and learning in postsecondary education, to illuminate the context that shapes these new directions, to illustrate these new directions through examples from real settings, and to propose ways in which these new directions can be incorporated into still other settings.

This publication reflects the view that teaching deserves respect as a high form of scholarship. We believe that significant scholarship is conducted not only by researchers who report results of empirical investigations but also by practitioners who share disciplinary reflections about teaching. Contributors to NDTL approach questions of teaching and learning as seriously as they approach substantive questions in their own disciplines, and they deal not only with pedagogical issues but also with the intellectual and social context in which these issues arise. Authors deal on the one hand with theory and research and on the other with practice, and they translate from research and theory to practice and back again.

About This Volume

This volume focuses on the research and practice associated with a model for motivation, volition, and performance (MVP model). Readers will appreciate the framework that this model provides as they choose appropriate teaching and learning pedagogies in their courses and beyond. This volume provides theoretical constructs and applications of the MVP model that will be useful to anyone who is interested in improving and enhancing student learning.

Catherine Wehlburg
Editor-in-Chief

Catherine M. Wehlburg is the associate provost for institutional effectiveness at Texas Christian University.

CONTENTS

9. Summary and Recommendations 109
Michael Theall, John M. Keller
This brief chapter outlines themes and ideas drawn from this issue.

INDEX 113

Memorium and Dedication

All of us who are responsible for various parts of this document were extremely saddened to learn of Professor Michael Theall's death during the final stages of its development and production. It was Mike's concept, enthusiasm, and drive that led to the creation of this thematic issue. We were happy that he got to see and react to all of the chapter contents before his untimely and sad passing. We pray for his widow, Louise, who was by his side during the whole process and wish to dedicate this document to her.

Published online in Wiley Online Library (wileyonlinelibrary.com). • DOI: 10.1002/tl.20275

Editors' Notes

Michael Theall, John M. Keller

Motivation has been the subject of research for decades and has been investigated and applied in fields as varied as psychology, education, business, sociology, neuroscience, and communications. In education at all levels, motivation—or more specifically, motivating students—has been stated as a primary goal. However, simply saying that teachers should motivate students ignores both the complexity of that activity and a larger group of equally important topics, especially the conditions and environments in which teaching and learning take place.

One well-known response to these issues is Keller's motivational design of instruction strategy and its general attention, relevance, confidence, and satisfaction (ARCS) model. The model is widely recognized and used in K–12 education but has not been as widely incorporated into higher education practice. This New Directions issue focuses on Keller's extension of the ARCS model to a new form that acknowledges the importance of volition as action subsequent to motivation: action that leads to improved performance. This motivation, volition, and performance (MVP) model provides a framework for considering various teaching and learning topics and can be extended into other areas such as professional development and evaluation. The chapters outlined here provide concrete ideas for integrating and using the MVP model.

Part 1: Foundations

In Chapter 1, John M. Keller provides an overview of the MVP model and discusses the links between motivation, volition, performance, and contextual and individual difference variables.

In Chapter 2, Todd Zakrajsek considers neuroscience, brain function, and the importance of emotion in learning and discusses how the MVP model might be applied as a framework for capitalizing on this emerging knowledge. How can faculty design instruction that connects positive emotional outcomes and strategies that support learner interests, the initiation of volitional activity and self-regulation, and improved performance?

Part 2: Applications

In Chapter 3, Jennifer L. Franklin considers instructional design, the unique aspects of online learning, and how use of the MVP model might help online learners stay on task, organize and plan their work, and successfully complete coursework. Franklin also describes how new technologies and the online environment offer unique affordances that can be used to address obstacles to online teaching and learning and to allow effective assessment.

In Chapter 4, DeBorah D. Graham and Michael Theall discuss learners' development of professional values and attitudes in teacher education programs. Many disciplines have curricula that emphasize these "dispositions" and there are three primary concerns: (1) engaging students in introductory courses, (2) sustaining this interest and promoting self-regulation, and (3) determining how to assess learning outcomes. The authors relate the MVP model to these concerns and propose ideas for providing a consistent focus on intended course outcomes and on understanding, acceptance, and adoption of professional dispositions.

In Chapter 5, Karen A. Becker relates the MVP model to twenty years of experience in developing and teaching college survival skills in a Reading and Study Skills program, and demonstrates how deliberate attention to MVP can lead to sustained motivation, volitional action, and academic success. Successful patterns of motivation and volition established in early college courses promote success, satisfaction, and importantly, better retention.

In Chapter 6, Marilla D. Svinicki uses the MVP model in a different way. Acknowledging that learners are not the sole focus of motivational activities and programs, she considers how professionals in instructional design and faculty development roles can support faculty efforts to help learners become and remain motivated. She reviews several traditional faculty development strategies and offers suggestions about how and why these strategies can be effective in sustaining faculty motivation and volition. Professional development programs and careful faculty evaluation can help faculty to advance and sustain their careers. The issue is not simply motivating faculty, but (as is the case in many professional development contexts) following up initial activities and events with ongoing programs that promote willful action.

In Chapter 7, Michael Theall provides a parallel to Chapter 6 by considering the MVP model with respect to faculty evaluation. This chapter acknowledges the motivational impact of good versus bad evaluation practice. This discussion includes notes on the most controversial aspect of faculty evaluation: the use of student ratings of instruction. Ratings are not evaluations, the author says, because evaluations are actually done by those who review data in order to make decisions about performance. The chapter concludes with recommendations for improved practice that supports motivation, volition, and performance.

Part 3: Outcomes

In Chapter 8, Thomas A. Angelo brings the MVP model and assessment principles together and reviews strategies for preparing measurable learning outcome statements and determining if instructional and motivational strategies have been successful. Teaching and learning in the affective domain pose unique problems with respect to assessment. Even if leaners are motivated at entry, and begin volitional activity such as self-regulation, what can happen in a real-world or workplace environment that can reduce or extinguish motivation? In other words, does positive evidence at the end of a course or program mean that the desired outcomes will continue?

In Chapter 9, John M. Keller and Michael Theall review the issue with specific focus on the integration and application of the MVP model. This section identifies themes and underlying relationships in the chapter applications that point to the potential value of careful consideration of the MVP model when college courses are designed and presented and to a better understanding of how to assess teachers' and learners' success in higher education.

MICHAEL THEALL is emeritus professor of education, Youngstown State University.

JOHN M. KELLER is professor emeritus of the Department of Educational Psychology and Learning Systems, Florida State University.

1

This chapter contains an overview of the MVP model that is used as a basis for the other chapters in this issue. It also contains a description of key steps in the ARCS-V design process that is derived from the MVP model and a summary of a design-based research study illustrating the application of the ARCS-V model.

The MVP Model: Overview and Application

John M. Keller

According to the principle of Occam's razor, simplicity is a virtue. Simpler theories are preferable to more complex ones because they have fewer assumptions and it is easier to test their validity. However, some situations are inherently complex and even the simplest explanations can be challenging. In the present case, I provide a theory of motivation, volition, and performance (MVP; Keller 2008) that is somewhat complex because it integrates research and theory to provide guidance for instructional designers who wish to develop comprehensive and ecologically valid programs of instruction. This theory is represented in a system model provided in this chapter. Even though the overall theory is complex, it follows a logical progression when you approach it one section at a time. This chapter contains a summary of the MVP model with an emphasis on its motivational and volitional components together with a systematic motivational design process for applying the model to many types of learning environments. An overview of the model is followed by a description of the ARCS-V design process and a case example of its application.

The Long History of Motivation

Efforts to understand human motivation are centuries old. For example, in the opening paragraph of *Metaphysics*, Aristotle stated, "All men [sic] by nature desire to know," and he then explored the implications of this assumption about the inherent nature of curiosity. But, in the context of psychology, motivation was for many years defined as a person's reactive response to external stimuli rather than as a propelling force. This conceptualization has often been characterized metaphorically as the "carrot or

New Directions for Teaching and Learning, no. 152, Winter 2017 © 2017 Wiley Periodicals, Inc.
Published online in Wiley Online Library (wileyonlinelibrary.com) • DOI: 10.1002/tl.20265

stick" approach that assumes giving rewards for correct behavior increases the occurrence of that behavior and administering punishment for unacceptable behavior decreases its occurrence. But punishment does not have as high a success rate as rewards. The carrot or stick approach explains numerous facets of motivation but there are many aspects including desire, goals, and persistence that it does not explain. A definition that is inclusive enough to contain all of these characteristics was provided by Keller (1983) who proposed that motivation is that which explains the direction, magnitude, and persistence of behavior. This is more of a propelling approach that is closer to Aristotle's assumption.

The MVP Model and ARCS-V

The genesis of this definition and its evolution into the MVP theory began years ago when I attempted to synthesize motivational concepts and theories in a parsimonious, valid, and practical way. This synthesis would be theoretically valid and also provide a basis for designing successful motivational interventions given that there was no adequate guidance for designing the motivational aspects of instruction. There were myriad theories that pertained to total design but no models that incorporated all of the relevant variables. This task became the focus of an advanced graduate seminar that I led on the topic of motivation and learning. The result was a four component model that resulted from listing as many motivational constructs as we could find and then aggregating them into groups by means of a qualitative cluster analysis in which we combined constructs based on shared attributes. Four clusters emerged (Keller 1983) and became known as the attention, relevance, confidence, and satisfaction (ARCS) model (Keller 1984). Thanks to the influence of a German colleague, this theory was expanded to include the concept of volition, which now makes it ARCS–V (Keller 2008). Elaborations of the following concepts together with scholarly citations can be found in Keller (2010).

Attention. The attention category incorporates research on curiosity and arousal, interest, boredom, and other related areas such as sensation seeking. These concepts illustrate the importance of incorporating a variety of tactics to gain learner attention by the use of interesting graphics and animations, visual or verbal scenarios that introduce incongruity or conflict, mystery, unresolved problems, and other techniques to stimulate a sense of inquiry in the learners. It is also important to incorporate variability in one's approaches, because no matter how interesting a given tactic is, people will adapt to it and lose interest over time.

Relevance. The second category, relevance, refers to learners' perceptions that the instructional requirements are consistent with their goals, compatible with their learning styles, and connected to their past experiences. A key component of relevance is goal orientation, which, as demonstrated in traditional achievement motivation research, has been proven to facilitate motivation and achievement. Learner goals can be extrinsically motivated, as illustrated by the need to pass a course to be eligible for a desired opportunity, or intrinsically motivated as when the learner is engaged in actions that are personally interesting and freely chosen. This condition of intrinsic motivation is an example of self-determination, which leads to sustained goal-oriented behavior.

Confidence. The third category, confidence, refers to the effects of positive expectancies for success, experiences of success, and attributions of successes to one's own abilities and efforts rather than to luck, chance, or task difficulty (too easy or too difficult). This is accomplished by helping students establish positive expectancies for success. For example, students often have low confidence because they have very little understanding of what is expected of them. It is easier to build confidence by making the objectives clear and providing examples of acceptable achievements. Another aspect of confidence is how one attributes the causes of successes or failures. Being successful in one situation can improve overall confidence if the person attributes success to personal effort or ability. But, if students believe that success was a result of external factors such as luck, lack of challenge, or decisions of other people, then confidence in their skills is not likely to increase.

Satisfaction. If the learners are attentive, interested in the content, and moderately challenged, then they will be motivated to learn. But to sustain this motivation, the fourth condition of motivation, satisfaction, is required. It refers to positive feelings about accomplishments and learning experiences. It means that students receive recognition and evidence of success that supports their intrinsic feelings of satisfaction and their judgment that they believe they have been treated fairly. Tangible extrinsic rewards can also produce satisfaction and they can be either substantive or symbolic. That is, they can consist of grades, privileges, promotions, or such things as certificates or other tokens of achievement. Opportunities to apply what one has learned coupled with personal recognition support intrinsic feelings of satisfaction. Finally, a sense of equity, or fairness, is important. Students must feel that the amount of work required by the course was appropriate, that there was internal consistency between objectives, content, and tests and that there was no favoritism in grading. Thus, there are both cognitive and emotional aspects to feelings of satisfaction.

Volition. Although the ARCS model has been validated and applied, it is limited by certain assumptions about motivation and persistence. One of the conceptual foundations of the ARCS model is expectancy-value theory, which postulates that people will be motivated to pursue a goal if it has high perceived value and they expect it to be achievable. This theory presumes that high levels of motivation will result in persistent efforts to achieve the desired goal, but this isn't always true because various kinds of distractions, obstacles, and competing goals can interfere with persistence. People who are able to overcome these obstacles and maintain their goal-oriented intentions tend to employ volitional (Kuhl 1987), or self-regulatory (Zimmerman 2002), strategies that help them stay on task. All of these strategies pertain to the problem of maintaining goal-oriented behavior and overcoming discouragement.

These five components provided the foundation for the final steps in the evolution of the MVP model, which was formed by adding information processing components and other cognitive and emotional components to illustrate relationships among motivation, learning, and performance. These relationships are illustrated in Figure 1.1, which is divided into six segments to facilitate discussion:

1. Attention, Relevance, and Confidence Motivational Components
2. Volitional Planning
3. Volitional Actions
4. Mental Resource Management
5. Information Processing
6. Satisfaction Motivational Components

The original ARCS components are in Segments 1 and 6, and volition is in Segments 2 and 3. Learning, as illustrated in Segment 5, results from a complex set of mental and psychomotor activities related to the acquisition, retention, and recall of information and behaviors. However, these activities do not stand alone in isolation from motivational factors that influence learning. Segment 4 contains factors that explain how a person's mental resource management governs the interactions between motivational orientations and both cognitive and perceptual activities that influence learning (see Keller 2008 or 2010, for elaborations). Effective learning strategies will incorporate the designed relationships related to mental resource management.

The six segments of the MVP model contain the primary constructs that explain the "Psychological Environment" related to motivation and learning. In addition, the MVP model contains a set of "External Inputs," which refer to the types of strategies that influence attitudes and behaviors. Designers and researchers build interventions by examining variables within these areas. Finally, the model contains a row of "Outputs" that provide a basis for measurements associated with the various types of effort, learning, performance, and outcomes related to consequences and satisfaction.

In summary, the five ARCS-V components of the MVP model provide a basis for understanding the various aspects of human motivation. However, understanding is not sufficient for motivational design. The question is, How do you use this knowledge as a basis for building effective motivational strategies? The answer is to employ the systematic motivational design process that was created specifically to accompany this model.

Figure 1.1. Components of the MVP Model

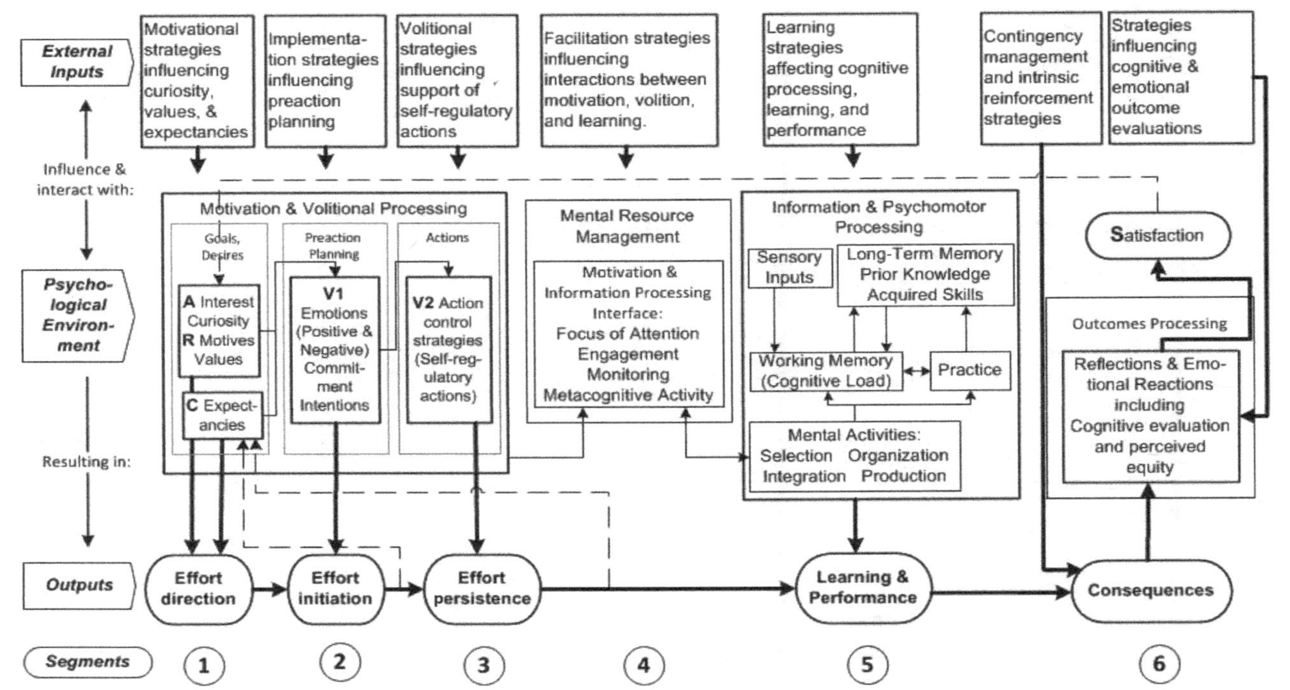

Applying the MVP Model: The ARCS-V Design Process

The purpose of the ARCS-V design process is to determine what specific motivational problems are occurring in a given situation and then to design strategies that target these problems. For example, the problem in a given group of "unmotivated students" might be that even though the students believe the content is relevant and they are confident that they can learn it, the instruction does not hold their attention. The ARCS-V design process includes an analysis procedure that helps you pinpoint the problem, and doing this makes it easier to solve the problem. There are ten steps in the overall design process (see Keller 2010, for complete explanations and templates with worked examples):

1. Obtain course information such as purpose and requirements;
2. Obtain audience information regarding background and reasons for taking the course;
3. *Analyze audience* to determine their precourse motivational attitudes;
4. Analyze other course elements such as instructional materials and environment with regard to their motivational properties;
5. List motivational objectives and assessments based on the identified motivational problems;
6. *List potential tactics* by brainstorming and collecting potential tactics related to the problems;
7. *Select and design tactics* based on a systemic review of the potentially useful ones;
8. Integrate with instruction;
9. Select and develop materials; and
10. Evaluate and revise.

Steps 3, 6, and 7 are critical. Even though all of the steps are important, these three are most critical to the success of the design process, especially Step 3 because of its importance in identifying specific motivational problems to be solved.

Motivational Analysis. The goal of the analysis step is to identify your audience's motivational attitudes regarding a given course or other learning event such as an online lesson or a new module that you are introducing. One of the challenges in analyzing motivational problems is that we cannot think of motivation as simply ranging from low to high because it can be too high as well as too low (Table 1.1). When motivation is too low, students will not try very hard to succeed, and when it is too high, students may be overstressed to an extent that their performance is impaired. Thus, it is important to assess the expected motivational levels of students when you are designing instruction or preparing for a classroom experience. You can do this by simply reflecting on each of the ARCS-V motivational

Table 1.1. Indicators of Motivation Levels Being Too Low or Too High

Motivational Expectation	*Motivation Too Low Indicators*	*Motivation Too High Indicators*
Attention Readiness	Bored, daydreaming	Incessant questioning, agitated
Perceived Relevance	Indifferent, skeptical	Insecure, feelings of jeopardy
Felt Confidence	Helpless, uncertain	Smug, presumptuous, careless
Anticipated Satisfaction	Cynical, resentful	Unrealistic, disappointed
Volitional Habits	Ineffective planning, weak commitment	Obsessive, overcontrolled

dimensions and making judgments based on your past experience, talking with other experienced instructors, or using a questionnaire.

Analyzing each component of motivation will enable you to determine where there are major problems, if any. In this regard, we make a distinction between tactics and strategies used to sustain motivation versus enhancing it. Even if learner motivation is satisfactory in a given area, it is necessary to include tactics to sustain motivation because motivation is not a fixed characteristic: it will fluctuate over time. In contrast, there may be areas where there are serious motivational problems as when students perceive the instruction to be boring, they do not believe it is relevant to anything important in their lives, or they believe they are not capable of learning a particular subject ("I'm not good at math").

The focus in this explanation has been on learner motivation, but it is also important to analyze your own motivation because you are a key component of learner motivation! If you are not motivated and enthusiastic about the subject you are teaching, it is unlikely that the students will be. Many studies show that great instructors exhibit high enthusiasm (Patrick, Hisley, and Kempler 2000). But, enthusiasm is not enough. Analyzing your own attitudes will allow you to better modify them and better connect with students. An instructor's motivation level can be higher or lower than the students' levels. For example, a history professor might love the Middle Ages and get highly enthusiastic when she reaches that portion of a required world history course, but will her enthusiasm stimulate an equal level of excitement in her students? Probably not! But, by realizing that there is a gap, she can design strategies to create satisfactory interest.

Designing Motivational Tactics. There are several ways to transition from analysis to design by using the following two sets of questions (Table 1.2). One set is for self-analyzing your motivation and the other applies to your estimation of learner motivation. Additional tools and examples are available in Keller's (2010) motivational design book. Your replies to these questions will provide a basis for selecting and creating motivational strategies and tactics that will help you and your students to be more motivated.

Table 1.2. An Analysis Checklist for Analyzing Instructor and Student Motivation

Categories	*Instructor's Self-Analysis*	*Instructor's Analysis of Learners*
Attention	Am I excited about this learning experience and how I can make it interesting?	Are the learners going to be interested? What tactics will stimulate their curiosity and interest?
Relevance	Do I believe that this learning experience will be valuable for my learners?	Will learners believe it is valuable? What can I do to help them believe it is important?
Confidence	Am I confident in my ability to lead this learning experience effectively and interestingly?	Will the learners feel confident about their ability to learn this? What do I need to do to help them be confident?
Satisfaction	Do I expect to have positive feelings about this learning experience?	What can I do to help the learners feel good about their experience and desire to continue learning?
Volition	Will I provide effective supervision and support to the learners throughout this learning event?	What can I do to help the learners maintain their goal orientation and task focus throughout this learning event?

Where Do Motivational Strategies Come from?"

One response to this question is to use established strategy frameworks that you can adapt to your situation. Here are four frameworks that are frequently used.

Create a Felt Gap. People will not engage in learning unless they perceive a gap between what they know and what they want to know or need to know. If learners do not believe that there is a gap between what they already know and what will be taught, then you can use an opening activity such as a case study that will leave them with an understanding of where their gaps are. An easy way to do this is to give them a meaningful task that they cannot accomplish successfully without the knowledge or skills that they will learn.

Flip the Classroom. This approach is a very old instructional strategy that many educators have used frequently throughout their careers (see Joyce and Weil 1980 for models that incorporate the "flipped" concept) but has recently been popularized thanks to now being labeled as such and promoted (Bergmann and Sams 2012). Flipping consists of having students read the assignments and do an individual or online small-group learning activity before coming to class. Then, class time might contain a very short lecture and discussion to highlight key points and provide supplemental information from the instructor's experience, but the majority of class time would be spent on group learning activities that include such things as games, simulations, or problem-based learning activities. In this setting, the instructor becomes more of a facilitator and coach than lecturer.

Produce Problem-Based and Project-Based Learning Environments. Problem-based learning was created in a medical school setting in the 1960s (Barrows 1996). It is a student-centered approach in which groups are given complex problems to investigate. They use a systematic problem-solving process in which they identify what they already know, speculate about what they need to know, and then conduct research to obtain the necessary information to propose a solution. The instructor plays the role of a facilitator who provides support, guidance, and feedback but does not interfere with the students' own problem identification and solution activities. Project-based learning is similar except that it focuses on real-world problems and can be interdisciplinary. Two examples are: (1) students in an instructional design course are given the task of designing a needs assessment for a given organizational setting, or (2) medical students are presented with the problem of investigating the growing incidence of antibiotic-resistant bacteria and proposing solutions for managing the problem. As in problem-based learning, students work collaboratively to develop their approach and process for the project and the instructor works as a facilitator and coach in support of the students' work.

Transcend the Boundaries of the Formal Learning Environment. An example of this is provided by Small and Rotolo (2012) at Syracuse University who used social networking applications to more fully engage the students in class and to expand beyond the classroom walls. Students used social media, Twitter® in this example, to communicate with the instructor, other students, and even people outside the classroom who became interested in the topic and activities. Part of their motivation for incorporating Twitter was that it is an example of social media that are having a huge impact on our knowledge-based society. At first, they used Twitter discussions during face-to-face classroom meetings. Students were encouraged to bring their personal device of choice—laptop, smartphone, or tablet—to tweet during class. Using a class-specific hashtag (hashtags are used on Twitter to group conversations around a topic or event), students were asked to share their thoughts or questions anytime they wanted to, providing they were appropriate for the classroom context. This use of Twitter provided a "backchannel" discussion that augmented the class with tweets that included questions, comments, and even humorous observations that added levity. Students also shared links to additional resources related to the topic at hand, which helped to build competence. Another benefit was that people who were not even enrolled in the class would sometimes participate. For example, when the instructor was describing the use of blogs by a major corporation in the United States, the account manager for one blog began to participate in the discussion as did the author of one of the books they were using and other professionals who shared observations and comments. This type of activity helped students appreciate the content they were learning in the context of society, and it increased their interest in the topic. It also helped them become quite sophisticated in their use of this social networking technology. In their paper, Small and Rotolo (2012) describe ways in which they incorporated the ARCS model in designing the use of Twitter and described some of the motivational benefits exhibited by the students.

These pedagogical approaches have powerful benefits for motivating learners because they are based on real-world problems and stimulate serious, meaningful thinking and problem solving. In many ways, they model the approaches by professionals working in various fields of research and practice.

You can create a strategy portfolio for your own use or for the members of your team if you are in a collaborative environment. "Where," you might ask, "do you get ideas and 'recipes' for strategies that will be interesting and effective?" First of all, you have to want to do so! Instructors tend to focus on the content that they are teaching because this is their primary area of interest and they are intrinsically motivated by it. However, to build a good portfolio of motivational and instructional strategies, you have to look beyond content and become a student of your own game: the game of teaching. You can do this by browsing through books of teaching tips and strategies, learning to use media in creative and effective ways, and observing how people are teaching, not just what they are teaching. How do they organize content, especially when they use a technique that creates curiosity or drama? What kinds of interactive learning activities do they use, and what variety of ways do they use student-centered approaches such as group work? Then, in regard to approaches that you find appealing, ask yourself, "How can I modify these for my teaching setting?" This was exactly how I derived many of the strategies that were successful in my classrooms and workshops.

A Case Example of ARCS-V Design-Based Research

The other chapters in this issue contain examples of different settings and approaches illustrating research and applications related to the MVP model. In concluding this chapter, I describe an example of design-based research in which ARCS-V was applied by Dr. Janine Stockdale (Stockdale et al. 2008) during her doctoral research in the midwifery program at the University of Ulster in Northern Ireland. Dr. Stockdale points out that the World Health Organization challenges health professionals to increase breastfeeding rates, and in Northern Ireland, as in most places, the success rate in breastfeeding is lower than desired. Thus, the goal of her study was to develop and validate an antenatal and postnatal program of training and support for mothers. She incorporated the ARCS-V model in this process

Figure 1.2. Antenatal Motivational Profile of Mothers Following the Original Antenatal Breastfeeding Instruction

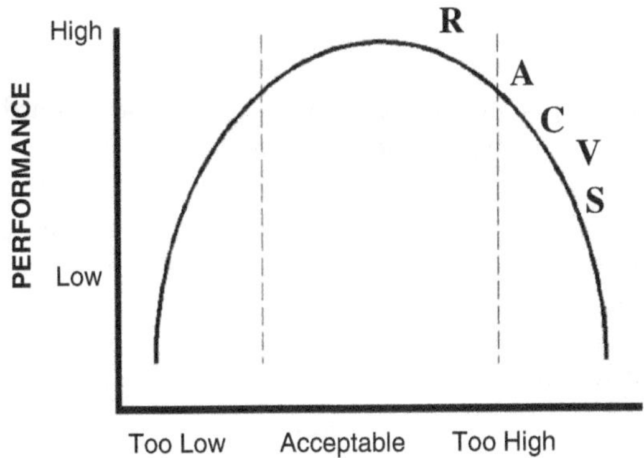

because motivational issues are presumed to play a dominant role in the compliance or noncompliance behavior of the mothers. For the purpose of this example, I have added the "V" component to illustrate the full model.

In Northern Ireland, mothers-to-be typically attend a workshop prior to giving birth (an antenatal workshop) and then, following birth, they receive postnatal support that includes home visits from the midwife. Dr. Stockdale's goal was to identify specific problems in the attitudes of the mothers and the behaviors of the midwives that negatively affected breastfeeding compliance. And then, after evaluating the existing antenatal workshop, her next step was to improve it together with other aspects of support. In her project, she established a baseline set of measures by analyzing the motivational attitudes of the mothers after they attended the antenatal instructional program on breastfeeding. Then, she measured them again during the postnatal period. An instrument called the "Course Interest Survey" (Keller 2010) was modified to fit this setting. After revising and implementing the antenatal workshop and elements of the postnatal support system, she measured mothers' attitudes again to determine if there were changes.

The mothers' attitudes following the original antenatal workshop are portrayed on the inverted-U curve in Figure 1.2. This graph is not a mathematical model but it illustrates an approximation of the magnitude of each of the five elements. These results revealed that the mothers were, overall, too optimistic about how easy breastfeeding would be and how great they would feel. More specifically:

1. Attention was slightly elevated. During the instruction, mothers were keenly attentive and received frequent reminders about breastfeeding characteristics;
2. Relevance was on the high side of satisfactory. Many of the mothers would make comments such as "It is important to me," and "It is

very meaningful to me." Some midwives made more negative or threatening comments to illustrate the relevance of breastfeeding. "If you don't breastfeed, you could get breast cancer," and "Bottle feeding will cost you £1600 every year";

3. Confidence was slightly elevated. "It will feel comfortable";
4. Satisfaction expectations were too high. "I look forward to breastfeeding," and "Most people who breastfeed feel a great sense of personal satisfaction";
5. Volitional expectations were also elevated. Many mothers expected that it would be easy to persist. "Most women find breastfeeding plain [smooth] sailing."

During the postnatal period following the original instruction, some mothers were very successful and expressed positive attitudes on all five dimensions of the ARCS-V model. However, the number of mothers who were not successful was substantially higher than desired and Dr. Stockdale conducted an analysis of these mothers and found:

1. Attention diminished. Many mothers found that instead of being attentive to the baby, their attention would wander as they reflected on their experience. "I frequently think of quitting breastfeeding."
2. Relevance was reduced. They began to reject some of their antenatal attitudes about the value of breastfeeding and found alternatives to be acceptable. "Bottle feeding has been adequate for thousands and thousands of mothers and babies."
3. Confidence decreased. They found the challenges to be too great. "It is painful and uncomfortable."
4. Satisfaction decreased. They were not happy about the experience. "Generally speaking I am not very satisfied with breastfeeding."
5. Volition decreased. They gave up on their efforts to be persistent "Breastfeeding just doesn't fit in with my schedule."

Figure 1.3 summarizes results.

Based on these results, she enhanced the antenatal instruction. She found that the original instruction included both positive and negative motivational guidance (positive feelings for doing it and negative consequences for not doing it). The original class also included direct instruction with examples but sometimes included misconceptions and inaccuracies from the midwives themselves. She revised the antenatal instruction by avoiding negative motivation and lowering fear of failure by including realistic consideration of the problems that can and often do occur and how to solve them. She also improved the postnatal support system by adding more modeling, more emphasis on attributing positive events to the mothers' efforts and abilities, and providing noncritical acceptance of mothers' decisions to switch to bottles. Collectively, these enhancements were packaged in

Figure 1.3. Postnatal Motivational Profile of Mothers Following the Original Antenatal Breastfeeding Instruction

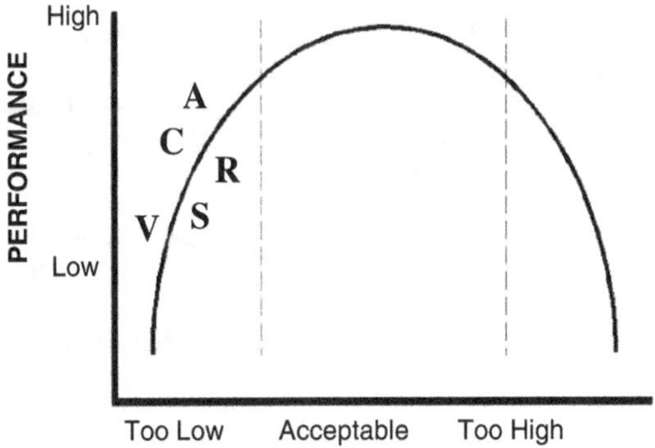

a program called "Designer Breastfeeding" (Stockdale et al. 2008), and it was found to significantly improve breastfeeding experiences and success rates.

Summary

In settings where systematic design is used as part of the problem identification and problem-solving processes, people often strive to build algorithms based on straightforward cause and effect relationships. For example, "if the problem is X, then the solution is Y," "If you do X, then Y will follow." This level of prescription can be approximated if not achieved in some areas of managing human behavior. For example, distributed practice is better than massed practice for effective learning. Administering positive reinforcement will normally increase the frequency of the rewarded behavior. But, as I indicated at the beginning of this chapter and as is obvious to anyone actively involved in trying to influence people's learning and performance, teaching and other behavioral change interventions can seldom be this mechanistic. At best, we can offer guidance and heuristics that are helpful but still require insight and active problem solving on the part of the teacher or other behavior change agent. It is this type of support that is offered by the MVP theory and the ARCS-V systematic design process. These models help you identify the areas in which you are already succeeding as a motivating designer or teacher and those areas in which you can make improvements. As illustrated in this chapter, MVP and ARCS-V models provide a means to design research and practices based on a systematic analysis of motivational characteristics. Basic inquiry on variables related to the model and on design-based research are supported by these models.

References

Barrows, Howard S. 1996. "Problem-Based Learning in Medicine and Beyond: A Brief Overview." In *Bringing Problem-Based Learning to Higher Education: Theory and Practice*, New Directions for Teaching and Learning, no. 68, edited by Luann Wilkerson and Wim H. Gijselaers, 3–13. San Francisco: Jossey-Bass.

Bergmann, Jonathan, and Aaron Sams. 2012. *Flip Your Classroom: Reach Every Student in Every Class Every Day*. New York: ISTE and ASTD.

Joyce, Bruce, and Marsha Weil. 1980. *Models of Teaching*, 2nd ed. Englewood Cliffs, NJ: Prentice-Hall, Inc.

Keller, John M. 1983. "Motivational Design of Instruction." In *Instructional Design Theories and Models: An Overview of their Current Status*, edited by Charles M. Reigeluth, 383–433. Hillsdale, NJ: Lawrence Erlbaum Associates.

Keller, John M. 1984. "The Use of the ARCS Model of Motivation in Teacher Training." In *Aspects of Educational Technology. Vol. XVII: Staff Development and Career Updating*, edited by Ken E. Shaw and Andrew J. Trott. London: Kogan Page.

Keller, John M. 2008. "An integrative Theory of Motivation, Volition, and Performance." *Technology, Instruction, Cognition, and Learning* 6(2): 79–104.

Keller, John M. 2010. *Motivational Design for Learning and Performance: The ARCS Model Approach*. New York: Springer.

Kuhl, Julius 1987. "Action Control: The Maintenance of Motivational States." In *Motivation, Intention and Volition*, edited by Frank Halisch and Julius Kuhl, 279–291. Berlin: Springer.

Patrick, Brian C., Jennifer Hisley, and Toni Kempler. 2000. "'What's Everybody So Excited About?': The Effects of Teacher Enthusiasm on Student Intrinsic Motivation and Vitality." *Journal of Experimental Education* 68(3): 217–236.

Small, Ruth V., and Anthony Rotolo. 2012. "Motivating Learning Engagement through Social Media Both *in* and *on* the Enterprise." *Future Learning* 1(1): 33–42.

Stockdale, Janine, Marlene Sinclair, W. George Kernohan, John M. Keller, Lynn Dunwoody, Joseph B. Cunningham, Lorna Lawther, and Patricia Weir. 2008. "Feasibility Study to Test Designer Breastfeeding^{TM}: a Randomised Controlled Trial." *Evidence Based Midwifery* 6(3): 76–82.

Zimmerman, Barry J. 2002. "Becoming a Self-Regulated Learner: An Overview." *Theory into Practice* 41(2): 64–70.

JOHN M. KELLER is professor emeritus of the Department of Educational Psychology and Learning Systems, Florida State University.

2

This chapter describes the ways in which the MVP model relates to recent research on neuroscience and learning, and demonstrates how those relationships may be used to better understand physiological impacts on motivation, and to facilitate improved learning.

The MVP Model as an Organizing Framework for Neuroscience Findings Related to Learning

Todd M. Zakrajsek

The motivation–volition–performance (MVP) model described by John M. Keller in Chapter 1 of this issue provides a much-needed frame of reference to make sense of the dizzying amount of research being conducted related to cognitive and social neuroscience and their relationship to learning. As an academically integrated and eclectic field, cognitive neuroscience brings together many fields (for example, psychology, neuroscience, physics, computer science, and biomedical engineering) in an effort to demonstrate the physical changes in the brain that occur as a result of learning. Social neuroscience is a related field that has as a focus the underlying physical aspects of interpersonal interaction. According to the Society for Social Neuroscience (n.d.) mission statement, social neuroscience "investigates the nervous system and its manifestations at many interacting levels—from molecules to societies—and brings together multiple disciplines and methodologies to define the emergent structures that define social species" (para. 1). Together, cognitive neuroscience and social neuroscience allow for the study of physical changes in humans as the result of learning and interacting with one another.

Neuroscience is a complex field based on a wide variety of systems. The complexity is augmented as each of the neural networks associated with brain-based systems have different functions. As a quick example, you may very well learn how to ride a bicycle (procedural learning) without ever fully understanding the physical principles that make the action of riding the bicycle possible. The differences between acquiring a procedure

Published online in Wiley Online Library (wileyonlinelibrary.com) • DOI: 10.1002/tl.20266

and understanding the actions involved make this an exceedingly important area in need of a conceptual framework.

To further demonstrate the complexity of human behavior, consider that it may be possible to learn a behavior without your knowledge that the behavior has been learned. This phenomenon has been recognized for a long period of time. Joseph LeDoux (1998) reports an "experiment" conducted in the early part of the twentieth century by a French physician, Edouard Claparede, who worked with a female patient who had lost her memory as a result of brain damage. Each day, Claparede would introduce himself to the patient, who quickly forgot who he was. He decided to try an experiment. He concealed a small pin in his hand, so she would feel a pin prick when shaking his hand. He was able to demonstrate that even though the patient with amnesia did not remember him, the next time they met, she refused to shake his hand. She did not understand why she refused to shake his hand, but she felt there was a reason. She had learned a response without any knowledge of having learned a new behavior. This concept has been demonstrated experimentally many times (for example, Brooks and Baddeley 1975).

Unfortunately, there are many misconceptions regarding the findings associated with cognitive and social neuroscience as applied to education. Although there are long roots to the study of brain-based learning, the field of neuroscience is relatively new, so there is some tendency to apply findings in inappropriate ways. Those working to better understand the brain and learning are becoming increasingly aware that humans process information in vastly different ways as a result of fundamental differences in the way neurological systems work (for example, Grandin and Panek 2013). Additionally, neuroscience is making progress in beginning to understand the educational process. That said, neither the student nor the teaching process has been the primary focus of the field. As noted above, some outside the field make grand statements that are often overly optimistic (Goswami 2006). Frustrated by the ready acceptance of many findings related to the brain, Stuart J. Firestein (2006), a Columbia University neuroscientist, began teaching a course on the concept of ignorance of scientific findings after noting that his students appeared to mistakenly believe that we know nearly everything there is to know about the human brain.

There do, however, appear to be connections between several findings of neuroscience and human learning and motivation. Keller (1983) includes in his definition of motivation the direction, magnitude, and persistence of behavior. These are key behaviors regularly studied by neuroscientists that hold promise in linking brain research to human learning. Volition is another aspect of learning that is included in Keller's model (Keller, 2008; Deimann and Keller 2006) and also has roots within neuroscience research. Within MVP, volition is the ability for an individual to maintain goal orientation and effort, even when faced with distractions and competing goals. Taken together, the concepts of motivation and volition form a foundation for how neuroscience may be used to improve our understanding of human learning.

This chapter uses the MVP model, specifically the concepts of motivation and volition, to better understand several recent findings coming from the field of neuroscience by filtering the plethora of current findings to better understand how they may interrelate and be better applied to human learning.

Motivation: Neuroscience Findings and Instructional Approaches Supported by the MVP Model

As noted previously, caution must be exercised with respect to applying findings from neuroscience to any aspect of teaching and learning. The MVP model, however, does provide a framework for anchoring some recent findings and identifying strategies and applications that might be proposed. Here are some findings related to motivation and volition and brief suggestions about how these findings can be used to advance student learning.

Establishing New Responses. Synapses are connections between neurons. Although some believe the number of neurons one has is primarily related to learning or knowledge, it is the connections among these neurons that are of utmost importance (Black 1991). We have approximately 86 billion neurons in our brain, and each one of our billions of neurons may have up to 10,000 connections. We may be so tired at times that we cannot learn, but overall, it is impossible to "fill" our brains. As we learn new information, our neurons establish new connections and when we fail to use connections, they disappear through a process called pruning. Essentially, our brains grow in areas of use and retract in areas of disuse. An additional finding is that repeated use results in a neuron pathway firing more easily. This process, called long-term potentiation, is one of the most frequently studied areas within neuroscience (Whitlock et al. 2006). As an example of the way long-term potentiation works, consider what happens when you get into your car each morning. You do not need to spend cognitive energy thinking about how hard to press the gas pedal. You effortlessly adjust the speed at any time with a glance at the speedometer. Over a long period of time, looking at the speedometer is less and less necessary, as the sound of the car becomes a primary indication of your speed. This is readily apparent if you drive a car that is quieter than the car you normally drive, in which case you may find yourself cruising along faster than you normally drive.

As a result of repeated action, long-term potentiation can even result in the formation of a habit. Barbara Knowlton (2014) notes that after a behavior becomes a habit, the action can be automatically elicited by some stimuli even when the outcome of the behavior is no longer considered. This means that even if there was originally a good reason for a behavior to happen—such as checking a term paper three times before handing in the work—after the habit has been formed, the established behavior of checking the work multiple times may well continue. Even when it is not necessary to continue the precipitating behavior to bring about the intended outcome—that is, turning in the paper—an established habit will continue to be a driving force. As well, even when in a new situation, if you experience a similar stimulating circumstance (for example, being asked to submit a paper for another professor, it is likely you will continue to engage in that same habitual behavior. Note that although this behavior may be maladaptive, it might also be extremely helpful. For example, when driving different cars, it is not necessary to learn that it is important to check the review mirror. That occurs out of habit.

It is relatively easy to relate this research to the MVP model in Segments 3, 4, and 5. Research pertaining to how neurons "fire" and result in behaviors or thoughts, has direct implications for the concept of volition. For example, behaviors that are practiced extensively have a physiological basis for being more likely to occur in the future through long-term potentiation and habit formation. Habits and easily firing neuron pathways are much easier to engage. Therefore, having students continue to practice recalling important information or engaging in important behaviors to the point of forming a habit or bringing about long-term potentiation is an important aspect of learning. Learning in this way is more persistent and information is much easier to recall. This leads to better performance and satisfaction (Segments 5 and 6).

Attention. There is a great deal of research in neuroscience pertaining to attention. It is also the first element in Keller's (1987) attention, relevance, confidence, and satisfaction (ARCS) model and it is embedded in Segment 1 of MVP. It is tempting to assume that to attend to something means to focus solely on that object or idea. This is experienced frequently while learning when you are told, "It is important for you to focus and to ignore everything else." Although focusing is important, one does not focus only on a specific stimulus or idea. In fact, too much focusing may hinder or reduce learning. Our brains are wired to quickly discount constant stimuli, as constant stimuli hold less information and are less attractive than novel stimuli. Moving stimuli have greater informational value than stationary stimuli. This is readily apparent if you take a walk in the woods at dusk. Trees blend to such an extent that you may not even process that they are all around you. At the same time, an object moving among the trees draws immediate attention. As movement and new information are more important than constant or static information, it is important to gather a variety of information at any given time. When one focuses on a photo, for example, research shows that the eyes look all over the photo. This [focusing] is biological. Paying attention does not mean unrelenting attention on one focal point. According to James Zull (2002), "Our brain evolved to notice details by shifting its focus from one area to another . . . . The brain is more likely to notice details when it scans than when it focuses. We exhaust our neurons if we make a constant demand on the same ones for too long. We rest them by using different ones for a bit and then coming back to the details that seem important" (Zull 2002, 142).

The ability to demonstrate volition by attending to stimuli is a developmental process. It is important to note that many college-aged students are still developing in this area. The brain does not reach full maturity until about age twenty-five, which means a great number of college students in classrooms have brains that are still developing. This makes it more difficult for students than it is for a more experienced faculty member to reason, plan, and even make decisions at times (Gotay et al. 2004). Aside from worldly experience, there is a physiological reason that college students struggle with reason and decisions more than we do as faculty. Ironically, the area of the brain needed to identify options develops sooner than the area that makes decisions. This means a student who engages in irresponsible behavior may be able to list appropriate alternatives but finds it difficult to decide which should be engaged.

Multitasking is another highly researched area within the general area of attention. Actions in which we engage may be placed along a continuum of controlled processing (needing great effort to complete) to automatic processing (behavior or thought that has been completed multiple times and therefore needs less effort). A behavior or thought that is a habit is an example of automatic processing (for example, $2 + 2 = 4$; the first president of the United States was George Washington; riding a bicycle). A behavior or thought that is difficult is a more controlled process (for example, driving a car during a snowstorm, mentally solving a difficult math problem, and listening to a lecture about a complex academic topic). For essentially every human, it is not possible to engage in more than one controlled process at a time. Attention to one item results in the brain essentially shutting down in the other area (Dux et al. 2006). This is an automatic process that aids attention.

If two controlled processes happen at once, there is evidence that the brain is essentially "designed" to shift from one item to the next, attending to only one at a time. Electrophysiological measurements have shown rapid changes in event-related potential in the brains of subjects who search for items within an array of options. Essentially, this is physiological evidence that we pay attention to items serially, not in parallel (Woodman and Luck 1999). This also lends support to the idea of "task shifting" rather than "multitasking" as the concept is generally understood. Research consistently shows that multitasking while engaged in academic tasks is detrimental to learning although some benefits of completing related multiple tasks simultaneously in everyday life can have positive outcomes (Carrier et al. 2015). On the negative side, however, there is strong agreement that some attempts to multitask are dangerous: for example, texting while driving.

It is important for students to clearly understand under which circumstances multitasking is possible and the detriments to task shifting when they mistakenly believe they are multitasking. Helping students to learn to attend to the most important aspects of anything they are learning can be very helpful. As an expert, you quickly recognize which items are most important. A novice must work diligently to acquire this expertise. Often a helpful concept is to model thinking for students, identifying which aspect you attend to and why attention is paid to one aspect and not another. In addition, it is helpful to explain the concept of limited ability for the human brain to attend to two controlled processes at the same time. Of course, one additional consideration is that the process of long-term potentiation and habit formation is one way to move something from a controlled process to an automatic process. Repetition leads to automaticity. When students say, "I have already learned this," a useful response may be "Yes, but you have not learned it well enough to make it automatic."

Affect, Empathy, and Social Contagion. There are obvious benefits to knowing how the brain is wired. It is beyond the scope of this chapter to delve into extensive physiological structures, but in the case of affect and learning, there is one that is directly applicable. Zull (2002) notes, "The outgoing connections from the amygdala travel primarily to regions of the cortex that are involved in the memory part of reflection (temporal cortex) and the creative and judgment part of abstraction (frontal and anterior cingulate). This suggests that the amygdala is set up to influence memory, ideas, plans, and judgment" (2002, 74). Because the amygdala is a powerful element in emotional reactions, there are strong links to MVP Segment 1 (where initial motivation can be affected by excitement about or fear of course content or performance expectancies) and to Segment 6 (where emotional processing of outcomes takes place). Given that emotions can affect one's desire or ability to make plans and judgments, MVP Segment 2 is also involved, and metacognitive activities in Segment 4 can be affected. Researchers in the area of social neuroscience have used functional-imaging experiments to report the phenomenon of humans coming to understand affective states experienced by others through neural structures that produce similar states in themselves. Essentially, by mimicking neuronal paths, humans come to understand one another through a physical mechanism (Decety and Jackson 2006). As Karen Becker notes in Chapter 5 of this issue, many underprepared students who are required to take "core" courses are not emotionally ready to undertake college work. Their fears can be compounded if other students are also unsure or negative in their expectancies. This relates to MVP Segment 1 in particular, and the affective state an entire class can be influenced. From another perspective, in Chapter 7 of this issue, Michael Theall notes that evaluation of teaching must be done carefully to avoid negative motivational cycles. If a large number of students in a class are fearful or negative, teaching becomes more difficult and it can affect student ratings of teaching, which, if low, can negatively affect the teacher who, in MVP Segment 6, is processing course outcomes. The high emotions so often a part of discussions of student ratings suggest that the social exchange of negative emotions in a classroom can have a strong, cyclical effect that does not help either students or teachers.

Researchers have identified neurons in the human brain that are much like mirrors to the world (Rizzolatti, Fogassi, and Gallese 2006). Although debate continues regarding the existence and function of mirror neurons, some researchers have identified very specialized neurons that may hold great promise in motivation and learning. These neurons are special in the way in which they are perceived to work. According to some researchers working with mirror neurons, when a person watches another person, a pathway in the observer is activated that is very similar to the person engaging in the action. That is, if you watch a person drink a glass of water, neurons are activated in your brain that are similar to those of the person drinking the water. Even more interesting is that if a person lifts an opaque glass and turns it upside down to show no water is in the glass and then puts the glass to her lips and pretends to drink, at that time different neurons are reported to be activated in the observer. That potentially means that neurons are activated in our brains not only by watching others but also by knowing the experience that person is having. If this holds true, it could be a physiological foundation for empathy. It may be mirror neurons or another brain-based mechanism. Essentially, everyone has seen young babies mimic adult behaviors. Mimicked behavior is also manifested in adults and has strong implications for learning.

Another physiological mechanism pertains to how we learn from one another by watching one another. Social contagion is a physiological occurrence whereby an observer is affected by the emotional state and actions of another human. Christakis and Fowler (2011) reviewed published work in the area of social contagion, reporting research pertaining to the "spread" of factors such as alcohol consumption, happiness, tastes in music, and obesity. Humans are greatly affected by the behavior of those in close proximity. Within classes, energy levels are an obvious example of this. If the instructor is interested and engaged in the material, students typically find the information more interesting. This makes sense as an expression of interest toward an object or idea signals to others, through contagion, that the object or idea is of value. This is related to the effect that can be demonstrated when one is standing outside and looks up to the sky. When this happens in a crowd, others will begin to look to the sky and the more people who look, the more interest it will draw from others. If you find course material uninteresting or boring, even without expressing that explicitly to students, your behavior can affect the class. It seems motivationally appropriate then, for teachers to model desired behaviors and habits of thought, and to evidence high enthusiasm for course content. In this way, teachers can promote "Effort direction" and "Effort initiation" in MVP Segments 1 and 2.

Sleep and Exercise. Sleep has been shown to be an important factor related to learning. Sleep is a very important time to transfer information from the hippocampus to the neocortex. This process is important in remembering learned material (Maas and Robins 2011). Individuals who are sleep deprived, or who have the last few hours of their sleep interrupted, do not establish memories as stable as those who are able to get a full night's rest. In addition to demonstrating the value of sleeping in the evening, many studies have shown the value of naps for academic learning. Researchers in Germany had students study fifteen pairs of cards. In one condition, students napped as part of the study and in another other condition students waited the same amount of time before recall (but did not nap). The students who napped remembered an average of 85% of the pairs, whereas those who did not nap remembered only 60% (Diekelmann et al. 2011).

Recently, research has been documenting the detrimental effect of blue light. Blue light is found in computer displays, eReaders, televisions, and many fluorescent bulbs. It is now well established that blue light suppresses melatonin production (Chang et al. 2014). This means that watching television, working on the computer, or playing a videogame on a smartphone before going to bed can make it more difficult to sleep. To combat this effect, there are applications on smartphones and filters for computer screens that block blue light in the evening.

Exercise has also been shown to be extensively related to learning. Although the relationship between the number of neurons and learning continues to be investigated, it is speculated that generation of new neurons likely happens for a reason. Researchers have found that regular exercise stimulates the development of new neurons, but not just anywhere in the brain. It appears that new brain cells that appear as a result of exercise develop only in the hippocampus, the specific area that is responsible for learning and memory (Ratey 2008). Exercise appears to also be responsible for stimulating the release of neurotransmitters responsible for attention, motivation, and patience. This provides another physiological basis for promoting motivation and attention in MVP Segment 1.

Sleeping and exercising during your class period will not increase learning. That rather obvious conclusion said, sharing information about sleep and exercise with students and helping them to understand the consequences of this information nonetheless holds great potential for improving learning. Within the MVP model, much of the research on sleep and exercise has tremendous impact on volition, attention, and performance. These issues are noted in Chapter 5 of this issue where Karen Becker describes a college survival course for beginning students. Becker stresses a body–mind–emotions (BME) connection and helps students to understand and adopt healthy, productive habits that support learning. Clearly, volition is a key here. Students must value these self-regulatory habits in order to use them consistently (as in MVP Segment 3 "effort persistence").

Conclusion

This chapter focuses on just a few areas emerging from the vast array of studies pertaining to neuroscience research with implications for teaching and learning. There are many physiological aspects to learning that have been documented, and the field of neuroscience is expected to continue to increase in popularity. There is certainly much we can do at a physiological level to establish new responses that are critical for learning content and establishing behaviors. As noted, the more frequently a neuron pathway is activated, the more durable that memory is over time. Additionally, strongly established pathways are the foundations for effective cognitive and behavioral habits.

Attention is another area noted in this chapter as having a physiological basis. Establishing and maintaining attention is necessary for the learning process to occur as it is impossible to learn when information is not attended to for a long enough periods of time for information to be encoded. Essentially, it is not possible to learn without encoding information, and it is not possible to encode information if the information is not noted. Attention is often divided by competing stimuli, and exercising volition to attend to the most relevant stimuli with respect to learning is a critical skill. Many believe students today are masters at splitting attention and still learning. Research does not support this position. Although it is possible to "multitask" in some situations, it is not possible to attend to two cognitively demanding tasks at the same time. It is likely most students would achieve more academic success if academic tasks were completed with more focused attention and fewer distractions.

Research in the areas of empathy, affect, and social contagion has demonstrated their importance in learning and memory. These concepts also have physiological bases that affect human learning. Social contagion and mirror neurons are also important in that they show a physiological aspect of human interactions as social animals. Social learning has a neurocognitive foundation and affects much of learning.

The final areas reviewed for this chapter were sleep and exercise. Although there is little one can do as the instructor with respect to these issues, it is imperative that students be made aware of the extensive impact these factors have on both learning and memory. Sleep and exercise also have a strong impact on attention, affect, and learning, making them exceedingly important in college and university life, particularly as these aspects of life suffer when study demands increase.

The MVP model provides a solid foundation to better understand the impact of physiological aspects of learning and also to suggest ways in which this information may be used to facilitate improved learning. Understanding how one learns is essential to becoming a better learner, and understanding that information in the context of an integrated model is particularly valuable.

References

Black, Ira. 1991. *Information in the Brain: A Molecular Perspective*. Cambridge, MA: MIT Press.

Brooks, David N., and Alan Baddeley. 1975. "What Can Amnesic Patients Learn?" *Neuropsychologia* 14(1): 111–122.

Carrier, Mark L., Larry D. Rosen, Nancy A. Cheever, and Alex F. Lim. 2015. "Causes, Effects, and Practicalities of Everyday Multitasking." *Developmental Review* 35: 64–78.

Chang, Anne-Marie, Daniel Aeschbach, Jeanne F. Duffy, and Charles A. Czeisler. 2014. "Evening Use of Light-emitting eReaders Negatively Affects Sleep, Circadian Timing, and Next-morning Alertness." *Proceedings of the National Academy of Sciences of the United States of America* 112(4): 1232–1237.

Christakis, Nicholas A., and James H. Fowler. 2011. "Social Contagion Theory: Examining Dynamic Social Networks and Human Behavior." *Statistics in Medicine* 32(4): 556–577.

Decety, Jean, and Phillip L. Jackson. 2006. A Social-Neuroscience Perspective on Empathy. *Current Directions in Psychological Science* 15(2): 54–58.

Deimann, Markus, and John M. Keller. 2006. "Volitional Aspects of Multimedia Learning." *Journal of Educational Multimedia and Hypermedia* 15(2): 137–158.

Diekelmann, Susanne, Christian Buchel, Jan Born, and Bjorn Rasch. 2011. "Labile or Stable: Opposing Consequences for Memory When Reactivated During Waking and Sleep." *Nature Neuroscience* 14: 361–386.

Dux, Paul E., Jason Ivanoff, Christopher L. Asplund, and Rene Marois. 2006. Isolation of a Central Bottleneck of Information Processing with Time-Resolved fMRI. *Neuron* 52(6): 1109–1120.

Firestein, Stuart. 2006. *Ignorance: How It Drives Science*. New York: Oxford University Press.

Goswami, Usha. 2006. "Neuroscience and Education: From Research to Practice?" *Nature Reviews Neuroscience* 7: 406–413.

Gotay, Nitin, Jay N. Giedd, Leslie Lust, Kiralee M. Hayashi, Deanna Greenstein, A. Catherine Vaituzis, Tom F. Nugent III, David H. Herman, Liv S. Clasen, Arthur W. Toga, Judith L. Rapoport, and Paul M. Thompson. 2004. "Dynamic Mapping of Human Cortical Development During Childhood through Early Adulthood." *Proceedings of the National Academy of Sciences of the United States of America* 101(21): 8174–8179.

Grandin, Temple, and Richard Panek. 2013. *The Autistic Brain: Thinking Across the Spectrum*. New York: Houghton Mifflin Harcourt.

LeDoux, Joseph. 1998. *The Emotional Brain*. London: Orion Publishing Group.

Keller, John M. 1987. "Development and Use of the ARCS Model of Instructional Design." *Journal of Instructional Development* 10(3): 2–10.

Keller, John M. 1983. "Motivational Design of Instruction." In *Instructional Design Theories and Models: An Overview of Their Current Status*, edited by Charles M. Riegeluth, 386–434. Hillsdale, NJ: Lawrence Erlbaum.

Keller, John M. 2008. "An Integrative Theory of Motivation, Volition, and Performance." *Technical Instruction, Cognition, and Learning* 6(2): 79–104.

Knowlton, Barbara. 2014. "Basal Ganglia: Habit Formation." In *Encyclopedia of Computational Neuroscience*. New York: Springer Science.

Maas, James B., and Rebecca S. Robbins. 2011. *Sleep for Success*. Bloomington, IN: Authorhouse.

Ratey, John. 2008. *Spark: The Revolutionary New Science of Exercise and the Brain*. New York: Little, Brown.

Rizzolatti, Giacomo, Leonardo Fogassi, and Vittorio Gallese. 2006. "Mirrors in the Mind." *Scientific American* 295(5): 54–61.

Society for Social Neuroscience. n.d. Mission Statement. https://www.s4sn.org/mission/

Whitlock, Jonathan R., Arnold J. Heynen, Marshal G. Shuler, and Mark F. Bear. 2006. "Learning Induces Long-term Potentiation in the Hippocampus." *Science* 313(5790): 1093–1097.

Woodman, Geoffrey, and Steven J. Luck. 1999. "Electrophysiological Measurement of Rapid Shifts of Attention During Visual Search." *Nature* 400(6747): 867–869.

Zull, James. 2002. *The Art of Changing the Brain: Enriching the Practice of Teaching by Exploring the Biology of Learning.* Sterling, VA: Stylus Publishing.

TODD ZAKRAJSEK is an associate professor in the Department of Family Medicine at the University of North Carolina at Chapel Hill.

3

This chapter is based on three premises. The first premise is that the use of instructional systems design (ISD) methods is important in online as well as traditional classroom settings. A second premise is that improving the motivational design of instruction brings benefits to teachers and learners alike. The third premise, specific to this chapter, is that new technologies and the online environment offer opportunities for enhancing motivation, volition, and performance (MVP) as described by John M. Keller in Chapter 1 of this issue.

MVP and Instructional Systems Design in Online Courses

Jennifer L. Franklin

Instructional design has always been described as a systematic process based on considering all the elements involved in teaching and learning. Although this basic reasoning is simple and appropriate, the actual process of designing instruction is complicated by the wide variety of instructional contexts, individual differences, and possible teaching strategies that exist. This variety makes it impossible to devise a single solution that fits all or even most instructional situations. In the case of this chapter, we now add to this complexity by acknowledging the impact of technology not only in terms of its capacity and sophistication but also the range of skills that users need and the resources required to help faculty and learners develop those skills. Finally, we include motivation and volition in the mix. As the editors of this issue state in their notes, it is insufficient to simply say that teachers should motivate students. Designing effective instruction requires consideration of all the factors that affect learning, and including motivational design requires attention not only to generating interest or curiosity but also to promoting learners' willingness to plan and then taking actions that lead to successful performance.

Instructional Systems Design

Early reviews of literature about designing instruction (for example, Reigeluth 1983) showed agreement about the basic process with a focus on the early identification of intended learning outcomes or, as Mager (1962)

New Directions for Teaching and Learning, no. 152, Winter 2017 © 2017 Wiley Periodicals, Inc.
Published online in Wiley Online Library (wileyonlinelibrary.com) • DOI: 10.1002/tl.20267

called them, "instructional objectives." Since then, many writers have presented models for instructional design. Diamond (1989) and Dick and Carey (1990) continued the emphasis with Wiggins and McTighe (2005) more recently using the term "backwards design" to emphasize the need to specify instructional outcomes before designing instructional strategies. The usual paraphrase for the overall ISD approach has been, "If you don't know where you're going, you may end up somewhere else."

ISD models have taken into account the current literature on learning and one influential outline was presented by Gagne, Briggs, and Wager (1985) who identified nine "events" that are involved in most teaching and learning situations. I have selected Gagne's Nine Events of Instruction for Table 3.1 as a point of reference because it is a prescriptive guide for effective instruction frequently offered to teachers, and it offers a set of principles generally followed to some degree by most trained instructional designers. In order to demonstrate the gap between high-level principles or generalizations about best instructional practices and the specificity of information needed to make actual design choices I have added questions an ISD professional would likely ask before committing to specific instructional methods. These are questions about instructional activities and materials that are necessary in order to enhance learning outcomes, and many of these questions are specific to motivation and volition.

The Motivation–Volition–Performance (MVP) cycle. The MVP cycle requires not only identifying final ("terminal") learning objectives/outcomes but also those behaviors and actions that allow ("enable") learners to achieve the outcomes. For example, Keller (1983), in his Attention, Relevance, Confidence, and Satisfaction (ARCS) model, notes that incremental success is important to sustaining effort. In the present case, Keller's MVP model Segments 1, 2, and 3 (as shown in Chapter 1 of this issue) refer to "Effort Direction," "Effort Initiation," and "Effort Persistence." These are terms derived from Kuhl's (1987) work on action control. Attention and relevance are incorporated into Segment 1, and planning and volitional action relate to Segments 2 and 3. However, there must be evidence of success along the way if learners are to gain confidence and so be willing to exert further effort. Thus, it becomes critical for teachers to be able to design assessments that allow them and their students to know what progress has been made and to make any necessary adjustments. In Chapter 8 of this issue, Thomas Angelo provides ideas for carrying out important formative and summative assessment specifically related to motivation and volition.

It is also important for teachers to do three other things. The first is to help students to develop deeper understanding of the learning and thinking processes that the discipline requires. This training can be done using strategies like advance organizers, concept mapping, and incorporating learning experiences that involve students in disciplinary and/or metacognitive processes. Recent emphasis on undergraduate research

Table 3.1. Gagne's Nine Events: Questions an ISD Professional Might Have Prior to Choosing Specific Approaches

Event of Instruction and Rationale	*Examples of Instructional Methods for Event*	*Examples of Questions a Designer Might Have*
Gain attention. Rationale: Gaining learner attention ensures the learners are ready to learn and participate in an activity.	Stimulate students with novelty, uncertainty, and surprise. Pose thought-provoking questions to the students. Have students pose questions to be answered by other students.	What might be novel or uncertain enough to surprise the kinds of learners for whom the lesson is being developed? How much surprise or novelty is optimal? How can surprise or novelty best be leveraged to enhance motivation (conversely, when does novelty undermine motivation)? How much or how often is attention needed during various phases or stages of instruction in order to help the learner stay engaged?
Describe the goals and objectives of instruction. Rationale: Informing learners of what will be expected of them better prepares learners to receive new information by establishing a frame or context.	At the start of instruction, describe what students will be expected to perform as a result of instruction by making descriptions of goals and objectives as clear as possible, by stating any intended learning outcomes in terms of actions, behavior, level or degree of success expected, and listing any relevant conditions under which the performance must occur. Help students make sense of new information by relating it to something they already know or to something they have already experienced.	What kind(s) of learning will be required (for example, cognitive, affective, psychomotor, volitional)? What specific kinds of performance are needed to demonstrate learning? What do students already know? What relevant experience have they already had with this subject or particular kinds of learning? Are there prerequisites regarding prior learning required for student success in performing these objectives? In what order should goals and objectives be presented and at what level of detail for optimal effect? Are there implicit sequences or hierarchies within the goals and objectives that need consideration? Does the way in which goals and objectives are presented affect motivation and/or volition? Are the goals clearly connected to content, instruction, and assessment? Are goals enabling or terminal?

(*Continued*)

Table 3.1. Continued

Event of Instruction and Rationale	*Examples of Instructional Methods for Event*	*Examples of Questions a Designer Might Have*
Stimulate recall of prior knowledge. Rationale: Helps students make sense of new information by relating it to something they already know or something they have already experienced.	Ask questions about previous experiences. Ask students about their understanding of previous concepts. Use a pretest that covers prerequisite concepts or skills. Use knowledge surveys.	What kinds of previous experiences are relevant to the new instruction (for example, school or career experience)? Have past experiences aroused interest and initiated effort direction and was this effort sustained leading to successful performance? If not, what happened and why? How likely is recall of prior learning experiences to enhance or impede motivation or volition? Does recall of past affective states as well as cognitive learning outcomes affect motivation or volition?
Present the material to be learned.	Use strategies to present and cue lesson content to provide more effective, efficient instruction. Organize and chunk content in a meaningful way. Provide explanations after demonstrations. Ways to present and cue lesson content include: – Present vocabulary – Provide examples – Present multiple versions of the same content for example, video, demonstration, lecture, podcast, group work – Use a variety of media to address different learning preferences.	Will presentation strategies enhance or impede motivation to learn? Will they interfere with or facilitate productive volition? Does the degree or type of structure in guidance affect motivation or volition? Is the essentially behaviorist/cognitivist approach to presentation/guidance/practice implicit in Gagne's principles more or less effective than a more constructivist approach? Does the source of guidance (e.g., teacher versus self) make a difference in motivation or volition? When does providing metacognitive guidance (learning to learn strategies) make the most difference in motivation, volition, or learning outcomes? How can the unique affordances of online learning platforms facilitate what kinds of learning? What aspects of online presentation of materials guidance enhance or undermine motivation and volition? How do individual differences in learners affect the effectiveness of various strategies for presenting information and guidance? Do the differences affect motivation and volition?

(Continued)

Table 3.1. Continued

Event of Instruction and Rationale	*Examples of Instructional Methods for Event*	*Examples of Questions a Designer Might Have*
Provide guidance for learning.	Advise students of strategies to aid them in learning content and of resources available. Methods to provide learning guidance include: – Provide instructional support as needed as scaffolds (cues, hints, prompts) that can be removed after the student learns the task or content – Model varied learning strategies—mnemonics, concept mapping, role playing, visualizing – Use examples and nonexamples—in addition to providing examples, use nonexamples to help students see what not to do or the opposite of examples – Provide case studies, analogies, visual images, and metaphors—case studies for real-world application, analogies for knowledge construction, visual images to make visual associations, metaphors to support learning.	
Elicit performance practice.	Activate student processing to help them internalize new skills and knowledge and to confirm correct understanding of these concepts. Ways to activate learner processing include: – Elicit student activities—ask deep-learning questions, make reference to what students already know or have students collaborate with their peers – Elicit recall strategies—ask students to recite, revisit, or reiterate information they have learned – Facilitate student elaborations—ask students to elaborate or explain details and provide more complexity to their responses – Help students integrate new knowledge—provide content in a context-rich way (use real-world examples).	What kinds of instructional activities can be used to elicit performance? How do these activities affect motivation and volition?

(Continued)

Table 3.1. Continued

Event of Instruction and Rationale	*Examples of Instructional Methods for Event*	*Examples of Questions a Designer Might Have*
Provide informative feedback.	Provide immediate feedback of students' performance to assess and facilitate learning. Types of feedback include: – Confirmatory feedback—Informs students they did what they were supposed to do – Corrective and remedial feedback—informs the student the accuracy of their performance or response – Remedial feedback—Directs students in the right direction to find the correct answer but does not provide the correct answer – Informative feedback—Provides information (new, different, additions, suggestions) to a student and confirms that you have been actively listening; this information allows sharing between two people – Analytical feedback—Provides the student with suggestions, recommendations, and information to correct his or her performance.	Does the source of the feedback (instructor, peer, or self-assessment) make a difference in motivation to learn or volition? How do the frequency and level of detail in feedback affect motivation and volition?
Assess performance to determine if lesson has been learned.	In order to evaluate the effectiveness of the instructional events, you must test to see if the expected learning outcomes have been achieved. Performance should be based on previously stated objectives. Methods for testing learning include: – Pretest for mastery of prerequisites—Use a pretest for endpoint knowledge or skills – Conduct a posttest to check for mastery of content or skills – Embed questions throughout instruction through oral questioning and/or quizzes – Include objective or criterion-referenced performances that measure how well a student has learned a topic – Identify normative-referenced performances that compare one student to another student – Embed questions throughout instruction through oral questioning and/or quizzes	How does the method used to elicit a performance of learning outcomes affect motivation and volition? What are the consequences of various levels of performance? Do learners get assistance in interpreting and processing results so that negative motivational cycles can be avoided?

(Continued)

Table 3.1. Continued

Event of Instruction and Rationale	*Examples of Instructional Methods for Event*	*Examples of Questions a Designer Might Have*
Enhance retention and transfer. Rationale: To help learners develop expertise, they must internalize new knowledge. Practice may be needed to apply internalized knowledge to new situations (future learning or job).	To help learners develop expertise, they must internalize new knowledge. Methods for helping learners internalize new knowledge include: – Paraphrase content – Use metaphors – Generate examples – Create concept maps or outlines – Create job aids, references, templates, or wizards.	Can retention and transfer be reinforced recursively to promote sustained motivation, volition, and effort? Can newly acquired knowledge be made more relevant by being linked to upcoming content requirements or necessary new skills, and can this connection also raise motivation to exert effort in pursuit of this forthcoming material?

Table developed based on information provided by Northern Illinois University at http://www.niu.edu/facdev/_pdf/guide/learning/gagnes_nine_events_instruction.pdf

reflects this kind of strategy. The website of the Council for Undergraduate Research (www.cur.org) contains information about projects, publications, conferences, and related events and services. Incorporating undergraduate research into the curriculum can promote motivation and volition. For example, engaging learners in this kind of research can incite curiosity and interest, add to the perceived value of the activity, and create positive expectations associated with getting involved in a challenging and even a "fun" project. These benefits are reflected in MVP Segments 1 and 2. The second thing teachers can do is to help students acquire a better understanding of their own learning and what the curriculum requires of them. In Chapter 5 of this issue, Karen Becker emphasizes the importance or providing such assistance to beginning students, especially those who may be at risk. This connects directly to MVP Segments 4 and 5. The third thing is to help students in processing and interpreting outcomes, the crucial activities identified in MVP Segment 6. Formative assessments such as "knowledge surveys" (Nuhfer and Knipp 2003) can be effective all through the semester and final assessments linked to course goals and instructional activities provide critical information about learning . In one sense, objectives targeting motivation and volition are really the means of enabling learners to achieve terminal objectives. This does not diminish the importance of motivation, but it does reinforce the notion that we cannot focus on only one of the systems involved when we are trying to systematically design instruction. We must think ecologically about the interactions of the many systems that comprise the teaching and learning processes.

Online Teaching and Learning. In online teaching and learning, the lack of face-to-face interaction raises questions about the extent and quality of interpersonal communication that has always been considered critical to teaching and learning. Thus, with respect to motivation and volition, there are important questions about how teachers can use technology's capabilities to replace traditional classroom communication and promote learner interest, action, and perseverance in pursuit of learning goals. Given that we are still learning about the dynamics of online teaching and learning, an equally valid question is whether the use of technology can actually improve communication and learning. Deimann and Keller (2006, 142–151) proposed Kuhl's (1987) conception of action control as important to motivation and volition and noted five obstacles to effective action control in multimedia learning that had been discussed by other writers: (1) a "serendipity" effect (finding something interesting by chance); (2), a "digression" effect (moving away from the target of a search); (3) a "navigation patterns" effect (difficulties keeping on track with program sequences and locations); (4) a "lost in hyperspace" effect (not being able to move ahead or to return to a prior part of a lesson; and (5) a "cognitive overload" effect (encountering more information than short-term memory can assimilate). I would add one more obstacle to this list: the lack of community in distance and online learning. In Chapter 6 of this issue, Marilla Svinicki suggests that the most effective motivational and volitional strategy in faculty development may be the Faculty Learning Community (FLC) idea developed by Cox (2001). One of its advantages is that individuals are supported by interacting with other FLC members on their joint projects. This mutual support sustains effort initiation and effort persistence (MVP Segments 2 and 3) and provides regular feedback on ideas and activities. The same could apply to online learners. In online environments, learners often do not have this kind of collaborative structure and thus try to go it alone—often with less success. The result is diminished motivation and volitional action especially when less-than-desired outcomes occur and are processed as negatives in MVP Segment 6.

Addressing Obstacles in Online Environments

The five obstacles noted by Deimann and Keller are interrelated in the sense that any one obstacle can compound the negative effect of another. For example, a serendipitous discovery while online can arouse interest or curiosity (MVP Segment 1) or effort initiation (MVP Segment 2) in search of related material, but this is a digression that takes a learner off task because of persistence in misdirected effort (MVP Segment 3). The search for other material complicates navigation by increasing the number of alternative digressions and increasing the chances of navigational errors. Haphazard navigation can cause a learner to waste time and to get lost. This result can lead a learner astray in terms of attending to the task at hand, marshaling the mental resources necessary to complete the task, and processing the information generated in the process. MVP Segments 4 and 5 are thus affected. The cognitive overload that results can further reduce effective effort direction and effort persistence, resulting in frustration and confusion: outcomes in MVP Segment 6 that can seriously degrade motivation. Because much online learning is individual, lack of community can make frustrations even greater. What does a learner do if there is nowhere to turn for assistance or even an opportunity to share experiences with a virtual classmate?

However, these obstacles can be addressed in several ways. Perhaps the common denominators in overcoming these obstacles are preparation, organization, and clarity. First and foremost, teachers and learners must be sufficiently knowledgeable users of the technologies being employed. Prior training, available support, and clear, understandable directions are crucial in terms of technology training but equally important in terms of course syllabi, course procedures, assignments, and assessments. These requirements reflect the ISD systematic approach discussed earlier (that is, consideration of all the systems involved) and interestingly, they are similar to the most important dimensions of college teaching identified by Feldman (1989). Even though Feldman's data came almost entirely from traditional classrooms, their connection to online instruction is apparent. The dimensions most strongly correlated with achievement were organization, preparation, and clarity. The next dimension in importance was the perceived outcome of instruction. This directly connects with expectancies in MVP Segment 1 as well as outcomes processing in MVP Segment 6. If learners (or teachers) expect to have technical difficulties or if help is not available, motivation and effort persistence (MVP Segment 3) will be reduced.

One other connection is important. It is the learner's perception of the value of the learning experience and the effort required to succeed. Perceived value relates to "Relevance" in Keller's (1983) ARCS model and falls in MVP Segment 1. Relevance is not simply a question of valuing a course because it may mean "getting a good job." It also concerns learners' perceptions of the subject matter and the innate value of the learning experience, and it affects learners' willingness to engage (that is, volitional action) in a course and its required work. Gillmore (1994) examined the number of hours learners spent preparing for class and the number of those hours they felt valuable. He found that the "time valued" correlated with student ratings of teachers and courses. Franklin and Theall (1995) further examined "time valued" and found that student ratings of instruction could be more accurately predicted in many disciplines by including the time-valued ratio in regression equations. They concluded that "concentrating on increasing the value of student time preparing for class could very likely benefit everyone" and that "success in increasing time valued... depends on faculty ability to improve the design, implementation, and delivery of the courses they offer" (1995, 47). Training faculty in implementing the ISD process is one way to achieve this goal and encouraging in-class or online discussions about how and why assignments and class work are relevant and important with respect to course outcomes is also very useful.

Serendipity and Digression. Given better technical preparation, teachers can help students to avoid serendipity and digression obstacles by providing limited lists of valuable websites and related resources and by limiting the amount and kind of effort involved. For example, a teacher might identify a small number of useful websites and instruct students to visit only three of those. Further instructions might be to report what was found at the three sites with respect to a specific question or issue. Students might be allowed to find one more website on their own and to report on that site as well. The assignment would require students to send the teacher brief descriptions of the located resources and their potential value (via any one of several technology mechanisms), which the teacher could then view and share with other students if the resources were sufficiently valuable. This process would limit endless and time-wasting searching and digressions and the reports would be measures of students' completion of the assignment as well as students' ability to locate and use resources. Sharing useful findings could also promote the development of a class affect: a "we are learning together" rather than an "I have to do it all myself" kind of feeling.

Navigational Errors and Getting Lost in Hyperspace. Although there is no way to control student "surfing" or prevent serendipity, having limits and specific instructions can at least reduce digressions, navigational errors, and getting lost in hyperspace. Importantly, the teacher's syllabus or other guidelines should emphasize why the assignment is structured the way it is and why and how the limits will allow more effective use of time and completion of assigned work. The time spent on these assignments can thus be more "valued" and motivation to complete the work will increase. This explanation will also improve the mental resource management and information processing activities identified in MVP Segments 4 and 5.

Cognitive Overload. Managing the ways in which learners use the technologies they have and providing structured guidelines for assigned work serve the additional purpose of helping students to avoid cognitive overload. Although the complexity of subject matter cannot be denied, teachers can use technology to provide mechanisms for coping with that complexity via tools such as graphics software for scaffolding or building concept maps and data or linguistic analysis packages. In writing-intensive courses, voice recognition word processing and bibliographic software has reduced the workload involved in preparing papers. Incrementally complex assignments that are recursive and/or link topics throughout the course will also avoid cognitive overload by reinforcing major points and the structure of knowledge in the discipline. Finally, incremental assessments provide opportunities for continued growth and enhance expectancy for success.

Lack of Community. New technologies allow for the development of community in several ways. User groups, work groups, and individual discussion areas are available in all course management systems and allow for focused dialogue and the exchange of ideas. These discussions can involve the entire class, collaborative work groups, or individuals. The teacher can monitor or participate in the discussions as necessary but is always a presence, keeping students engaged in focused discussion of course content. Social media, when managed and specifically connected to course requirements and assessment, can also increase the presence of a virtual community that reduces feelings of isolation. These can be supplemented with other resources such as telephone conversations and user-friendly technical support.

Technology and Assessment: An Important Connection

Arguably, skills and methods related to learning outcomes assessment are among the most critical in executing systematic instructional design because both the instructional design cycle and the learning cycle of students depend on timely feedback based on valid, reliable data concerning the learner's progress. Because motivation and volition are dependent on learner progress, one of the most underused aspects of online instructional technology is its capacity for allowing an instructor to monitor learning outcomes and learner behaviors.

High-level learning management systems such BrightSpace® and Blackboard® include novel and potentially powerful tools for defining intended learning outcomes in association with a wide variety of quiz and test formats and rubrics for evaluating qualitative data and student activity logging. BrightSpace includes a Competency feature, a robust framework for listing instructional goals and objectives that can be linked to specific measures using the Quiz and Survey tools or via externally graded measures entered into the Gradebook tool. The Rubric tool creates further opportunities for instructors (and learners) to formatively evaluate student work. Using the standard and custom reporting features, it is possible to cost-effectively monitor student progress with respect to specific skills, knowledge, or attitudes. Combined with activity logging, it becomes possible to see student work patterns and potentially identify needed interventions.

Beyond simply monitoring progress, BrightSpace makes it possible to give response-contingent feedback and clues that can make tests and exams opportunities for direct instruction as well as performance evaluation. Tools such as Checklist can make instructional content viewable based on whether a learner has completed a given activity or set of activities at specified levels of mastery. This has tremendous potential for regulating remote, asynchronous learning environments where students often wait for feedback to proceed effectively. Tools like these make it possible to see emergent motivation and volition problems (or success) in timely ways that can be hard to capture in classroom instruction, especially in large classes. BrightSpace has integrated the competency feature, measurement tools, and reporting tools intended to provide early intervention with predictive analytics and visual diagnostics to improve students' chances of success. Close integration with content presentation tools makes it possible to better understand how students are interacting with both instructional strategies and materials, and this, in turn, enables revision cycles to improve the course.

The ability to blend live, synchronous interactions with asynchronous, independent student work opens the door to adapting and implementing many instructional treatments commonly used in the classroom but provide the unique affordances for ongoing, automated monitoring that is not cost effective or practical in live instruction. Arguably, in large classes, the quality, frequency, and power of response contingent feedback can be amplified to new levels that may not even be possible in the traditional classroom. Assessments need not be limited to objective testing methods because the Rubric tool supports nearly any kind of performance measure. Other technology tools can be used motivationally or to track volitional behaviors, but in any case, it is critical to systematically link assessments to important learning outcomes.

Conclusions

Online teaching and learning present a variety of issues and questions that research from traditional classrooms cannot fully address. Using and ISD approach requires consideration of all the systems involved but retains the basic need to first establish clear and achievable outcomes. Teachers must distinguish between outcomes that are critical to learning course content and meeting the requirements of the discipline (the terminal objectives) and outcomes that are necessary along the path to success (the enabling objectives). Motivation and volition fall in the latter category for without attention to these issues, learners may not expend the effort needed to succeed or, even when well intentioned, may not manage that effort effectively. Because systems are dynamic, we must also recognize that no one strategy or solution will apply to all situations, all content, or especially all students. Individual differences among teachers and students can relate to skills, knowledge, attitudes, motivations, limitations, resources, or contextual factors, and the best way to deal with these factors is through ongoing monitoring and assessment. Fortunately, new technologies have provided mechanisms that make these processes easier and more efficient. In online instruction, the best of two worlds can be reached: teaching and learning that reflect tested theory and practice while retaining the interpersonal communication and interaction necessary to this most human exchange of ideas.

References

Cox, Milton. 2001. "Faculty Learning Communities: Change Agents for Transforming Institutions into Learning Organizations." *To Improve the Academy* 19: 69–93.

Deimann, Markus, and John M. Keller. 2006. "Volitional Aspects of Multimedia Learning." *Journal of Educational Multimedia and Hypermedia* 15(2): 137–258.

Diamond, Robert M. 1989. *Designing and Improving Courses and Curricula in Higher Education*. San Francisco: Jossey Bass.

Dick, Walter, and Lou Carey. 1990. *The Systematic Design of Instruction*, 3rd ed. New York: Harper Collins.

Feldman, Kenneth A. 1989. "The Association Between Student Ratings of Specific Instructional Dimensions and Student Achievement: Refining and Extending the Synthesis of Data from Multi-section Validity Studies." *Research in Higher Education* 30(4): 583–645.

Franklin, Jennifer L., and Michael Theall. 1995. "The Relationship of Disciplinary Differences and the Value of Class Preparation Time to Student Ratings of Instruction." In *Disciplinary Differences in Teaching and Learning: Implications for Practice*, New Directions for Teaching and Learning no. 6, edited by Nira Hativa and Michele Marincovich, 41–48. San Francisco: Jossey Bass.

Gagne, Robert M., Leslie J. Briggs, and Walter F. Wager. 1985. *Principles of Instructional Design*. Belmont, CA: Wadsworth.

Gillmore, Gerald. 1994, April 7. "The Effects of Course Demands and Grading Leniency on Student Ratings of Instruction." Paper presented at the 75th annual meeting of the American Educational Research Association, New Orleans.

Keller, John M. 1983. "Motivational Design of Instruction." In *Instructional Design Theories and Models: An Overview of Their Current Status*, edited by Charles M. Reigeluth, 383–434. Hillsdale, NJ: Lawrence Erlbaum.

Kuhl, Julius. 1987. "Action Control: The Maintenance of Motivational States." In *Motivation, Intention, and Volition*, edited by Frank Halish and Julius Kuhl, 279–291. Berlin: Springer.

Mager, Robert F. 1962. *Preparing Instructional Objectives*. Palo Alto, CA: Fearon.

Mager, Robert F. 1997. *Preparing Instructional Objectives: A Critical Tool in the Development of Effective Instruction*. Atlanta, GA: Center for Effective Performance.

Nuhfer, Edward, and Dolores Knipp. 2003. "The Knowledge Survey: A Tool for All Reasons." In *To Improve the Academy*. Vol. 21, edited by Catherine Wehlburg and Sandra Chadwick-Blossey. Bolton, MA: Anker Publications.

Reigeluth, Charles M. 1983. *Instructional Design Theories and Models*. Hillsdale, NJ: Lawrence Erlbaum Publishers.

Wiggins, Grant, and Jay McTighe. 2005. *Understanding by Design*, 2nd ed. Alexandria, VA: Association for Supervision and Curriculum Development.

JENNIFER L FRANKLIN is retired director of evaluation and assessment services, Office of Institutional Research at the University of Arizona. She is sole proprietor of ID&ES in Mt. Vernon, Washington.

4

This chapter discusses teaching and learning in the affective domain and the development of beliefs, values, and behaviors common in professional school education. We use Keller's MVP model as the basis for designing a teacher education course where professional "dispositions" are critical learning outcomes.

Using John M. Keller's MVP Model in Teaching Professional Values and Behaviors

Michael Theall, DeBorah D. Graham

Many disciplines in professional fields state that graduates should have acquired three things as a result of their experiences: (1) knowledge of the discipline's content; (2) skill in the practice of the profession; and (3) attitudes, values, and commitments that guide future professional behavior. Acquiring these habits and behaviors involves understanding them as well as incorporating them into value systems and day-to-day professional behavior. Although it is often said (too optimistically) that teaching disciplinary content and professional skills are relatively straightforward activities, it is also generally acknowledged—for example, by Barnes and Filer (2012) and by Duplass and Cruz (2010)—that helping learners to understand, adopt, and commit to long-term professional behaviors and values is a more challenging task. Assessing performance in these areas is also a complex undertaking because end-of-course assessment can address only current beliefs and attitudes and thus cannot easily predict what graduates will do in the future. Although learners can repeat what the desired outcomes are (because these outcomes are stated in most syllabi), this does not guarantee that learners fully understand the depth or scope of the outcomes statements or the actual in-practice behaviors that align with them.

Bell and Volckman (2011) and Kruger and Dunning (1999) have noted problems with learners' overestimation of their understanding of content, and this error can certainly apply to related information such as statements of instructional objectives. It is also the case that curricula in professional education often focus more on knowledge and skills in beginning courses but wait until upper level courses to observe and assess professional behaviors. If regular observation of new teachers were possible and practical over time, one would have to demonstrate that the presence or absence of desired behaviors could be attributed to the courses candidates took or to faculty member(s) with whom candidates studied. Nonetheless, accrediting bodies and professional organizations require emphasis on these affective areas whether the array of intended outcomes is called attitudes, values, dispositions, commitments, or behaviors. Even the most recognized guides for classroom assessment (for example, Angelo and Cross 1993) cannot provide easy remedies to the logistical and methodological difficulties faced in post-hoc assessment. Fortunately for readers of this New Directions issue, in Chapter 8, Thomas Angelo provides useful guidelines for assessing motivational and affective outcomes.

The Affective Domain

This chapter concerns the relationships of motivation and volition to achievement of instructional objectives that are in the affective domain and are associated with long-term professional behavior. Krathwohl, Bloom, and Masia (1964) presented the first taxonomy of teaching and learning in the affective domain. Objectives within this domain fall into five levels: "Receiving, Responding, Valuing, Organization, and Characterization by a value or value complex" (1964, 35). The levels are incremental and hierarchical, moving from initial awareness of the issues and stimuli that are presented to willingness to attend and respond to those stimuli, through the development of value systems, to the refinement of values via experience and/or new knowledge, and finally, to consistent actions and behaviors that represent the newly formed values aligned with professional standards. However, although the taxonomy has been useful as a framework for considering intended learning outcomes, it has not been widely used as a practical guide for designing and assessing instruction nor does it incorporate consideration of individual beliefs until the "valuing" and "organization" levels, where learners conceptualize and construct value systems. In professional schools, if the ultimate purpose of instruction in the affective domain is to help learners to develop beliefs and values that align with professional standards, there must be an early examination of learners' existing beliefs so that they can be compared to new knowledge and experiences and to those same professional standards.

Recent revisions of the original taxonomy by Neuman and Friedman (2008, 2010) include a revised model intended to help teachers design and deliver instruction. Their model has five levels: "Identification, Clarification, Exploration, Modification, and Categorization" (2010, p. 5). The first level is similar to Awareness, the first sublevel of Receiving in Krathwohl and others (1964), but rather than focusing on the learner's awareness of stimuli used in instruction, Identification is concerned with the learner's awareness and understanding of personally held beliefs and values and with the ability to articulate those beliefs. This is particularly important because the strength of existing belief systems has been known for some time in communications and social psychology literature (Rokeach 1960). More recently and from a different perspective, Zull (2002) described how neuronal networks in the brain are resistant to rapid change and knowing more about existing beliefs is necessary for effective instruction. He said, "So we might say that our best chance to help another person learn is to find out what they want, what they care about" (2002, 48).

Neuman and Friedman's (2010) Clarification does not have an equivalent level in Krathwohl and others (1964) but like Identification, is important because it requires review of the identified beliefs and values and an initial consideration of their validity. The third level, Exploration, begins a dialectic process in which new ideas are examined and compared to existing beliefs and values. This is a critical process because in instruction, professional standards can now be embedded in real-world situations that require learners to weigh the merits of alternative responses to those situations and to make choices of the most appropriate behaviors. The fourth level, Modification, is a process in which old and new ideas are synthesized and new alternatives can be proposed. Neuman and Friedman (2010) relate this level to the processes of assimilation and accommodation described by Piaget (1952). In assimilation, learners change new ideas in order to fit them into existing belief systems, whereas in accommodation, the belief systems may change as a result of incorporating new ideas. Accommodation is required when volitional action is a desired outcome. Finally, Characterization is very similar to the same-titled level in the original taxonomy. Learners have an organized set of values that is the basis for professional behavior, and they act consistently in ways that align with the values, beliefs, and standards discovered and developed during their courses and related field experiences. In many curricula, entry-level courses often focus on knowledge and skills, holding in-depth discussion of values and behavior until learners reach upper level courses. We do not suggest abandoning learners' development of solid foundations of knowledge in the discipline in beginning courses, but rather, we propose that early inclusion of strategies that promote reflection on affective issues and personal beliefs can be beneficial over the entire course of a program. Although this chapter emphasizes the affective domain, we feel cognitive considerations are equally important. A full discussion of the cognitive domain is not possible here, but we should note that early exploration of values fits into the revised taxonomy of cognitive objectives (Anderson and Krathwohl 2001) that outlines two dimensions: cognitive process and knowledge. The highest level of cognitive process is "creating." It encompasses all forms of creativity including the development of new ideas based on synthesis of multiple or conflicting views. The highest level of knowledge is metacognitive knowledge. It includes self-knowledge and knowledge that can be applied to a variety of contexts and conditions.

Motivation, Volition, and Performance

Clearly, for long-term success in these areas, there must be some initial motivational force(s) in place and these must be sustained over the course of study. These forces can be intrinsic or extrinsic. In *New Directions for Teaching and Learning* 78, "Motivation from Within" (Theall 1999), authors presented ideas about creating conditions that promote intrinsic motivation. The primary reason for this focus is that intrinsic motivation is thought to be more powerful than extrinsic, especially with respect to promoting volitional action. This belief is supported not only by various learning and psychological theories (Svinicki 2004) but by recent work in neuroscience. Zull (2002, 2011) says, "Emotion impels action. . . .Learning takes place through action but it is driven by emotion" (2011, 54). In other words, the will to act comes from within and has an important emotional component. A pertinent question is thus, "Where does the emotion come from?" Zull's extended discussions of the power of emotion (2002, 221–244; 2011, 53–80) note that learning itself results in a sense of accomplishment and the release of biochemical markers that are associated with pleasure and well-being, especially when the learner has expended effort (willful action or volition as used in this chapter) toward achievement of a learning goal.

A learner's curiosity or interest in a subject can provide considerable intrinsic motivation when that person begins a course. John Holland's typology of disciplinary characteristics and vocational choices (1997) notes that people make vocational choices on the basis of a match between their individual characteristics and the perceived characteristics of academic disciplines. Smart and Feldman (1998) point out that initial interest in a subject can either be accentuated or extinguished by the degree to which the learner's characteristics actually do match those of the discipline and by the extent to which the behaviors of faculty and other students in the discipline reinforce the learner's perceived person–discipline match. Having teachers as positive models of professional commitments and behaviors enhances this learning and is one part of the "accentuation effect" that Smart and Feldman (1998) refer to.

Extrinsic motivation can include such things as specific rewards promised by others for success in learning or pressure from family or peers to select a particular major field of study or from anticipation of a long-term reward such as a good-paying job after graduation. However, these kinds of motivation do not guarantee increased or persistent effort or improved performance. Extrinsic motivation can also come from useful individual feedback from teachers, or from traditional evidence of academic success provided by others, namely, grades and test results. Keller's model for motivational design of instruction (1983) and his motivation–volition–performance (MVP) model (see Chapter 1 in this issue) include the notion that both intrinsic and extrinsic motivation impact on effort, which in turn affects performance. Effort—especially purposeful effort like self-regulated activity aimed at the achievement of a personal goal (Pintrich 1995)—is often associated with enhanced performance, and the motivational consequences of successful performance can be powerful. The last part of Keller's (1987) Attention, Relevance, Confidence, and Satisfaction (ARCS) model is "satisfaction" and that strengthens motivation. There is abundant literature supporting this connection. Self-efficacy—one's belief in one's capability—(Bandura 1977) is increased, and a stronger sense of internal locus of control —the belief that one can influence outcomes—(Weiner 1974) results. Zull (2002, 221–244) discusses the positive emotional and motivational effects that come from being able to say, "We did it ourselves." In a related vein, Ricoeur (1992) proposed a process of "narrative emplotment" in which a person's experiences are woven into an ongoing narrative that makes sense of those experiences. Research by Hladkyj and others (1999) reinforces this notion and also connects with other attributional literature—for example, locus of control (Perry and Magnusson 1989; Weiner 1974) —and with "learned helplessness" (Seligman 1972). The narratives we build about our performance are powerful determinants of motivation and volition, and the motivational cycle can be said to be ongoing and capable of moving in both positive and negative directions. Although we might hope that students attribute failure to causes that they can successfully control in the future, this is not always the case. If the narrative includes a consistently negative attribution such as "I am just no good at math," motivation and willingness to expend effort can be significantly reduced or even extinguished. Fortunately, there is evidence (Menec et al. 1994) that these kinds of negative narratives can be changed through "attributional retraining" and effective instruction. These issues all connect directly to Segment 6 of the MVP model and provide input for continuation of the motivational cycle as described in Segments 1, 2, and 3.

The MVP Model and Teacher Education

Keller's MVP model has six segments, each of which outlines External Inputs, Psychological Environment, and Outputs. We discuss each segment with respect to its application in a curriculum that emphasizes affective domain outcomes intended to lead to the development and continuation of professional values, attitudes, and behaviors. We first provide a description of the context in which the model will be applied.

In teacher education, the National Council on Accreditation of Teacher Education (NCATE) long required that certain instructional objectives representing desired professional "dispositions" appear in all teacher education course syllabi (NCATE 2008). Now, accreditation is done by Council for the Accreditation of Educator Preparation (CAEP), and it has similar requirements. For example, CAEP Standard 3 section 3.3 states, "Educator preparation providers establish and monitor attributes and dispositions beyond academic ability that candidates must demonstrate at admissions and during the program" (CAEP 2013, 9). However, our observations and anecdotal evidence lead us to believe that many dispositional learning outcome statements are in syllabi as a matter of form and that the syllabi do not always present specific information about the intent of these outcomes. Although it is possible that some candidates are predisposed toward the desired attitudes, learners' acquisition of the dispositions must be a direct intent of instruction. When consistent, long-term behavior is a goal, preservice "candidates" and inservice teachers must be motivated to sustain professional attitudes and behaviors. This kind of commitment requires not only deep understanding of the principles that underlie the profession and allied value systems but also a desire to promote lifelong learning for themselves and their students and the willingness to engage in the self-regulation (Pintrich 1995) necessary in ongoing professional life.

MVP Segments 1, 2, and 3. In Segments 1, 2, and 3, the outputs are "Effort direction," "Effort initiation," and "Effort persistence." The three kinds of effort are critical to learning, and since the MVP model is dynamic and recursive, effort is influenced by events within the other segments of the model.

MVP Segment 4. Segment 4 deals with external input factors that influence motivation and volition, especially the relationships of motivation and information processing. Keller notes that "wishes, intentions, values, and emotions are part of working memory in addition to the traditionally recognized cognitive and perceptual components" (2008, 12). In Segment 4, activities within the psychological environment such as attention, engagement, and monitoring connect with learning and performance in MVP Segment 5. Keller puts these activities under the heading "Mental Resource Management" (2008, 11).

MVP Segment 5. Segment 5 deals with external input factors that affect cognitive processing, learning, and performance. This section parallels an essential part of Zull's description (2002, 13–18) of how Kolb's experiential learning model (1984) can be overlaid on the ongoing cycle of brain functions. Zull notes that input is received, identified, and integrated and then acted upon in the formation of plans for action that are then initiated. The consequences of that action form more input that is then treated in the same way as the cycle continues. MVP Segment 5 outlines the same sequence with learning and performance as outputs, and performance leads to consequences or outcomes that are also processed.

MVP Segment 6. MVP Segment 6 deals with outcomes processing. The external inputs are factors that influence emotions and the ways in which outcomes are evaluated, and it is at this point in the psychological environment that performance attributions (Weiner 1974) are made and narrative emplotment (Ricoeur 1992) takes place. These actions are particularly important with respect to affective objectives because negative consequences or even negative processing of positive consequences can have a major impact on the kinds of effort Keller describes in MVP Segments 1,

2, and 3. Although learning from one's mistakes can have many beneficial results, concentrating only on mistakes and creating a narrative of failure will reduce motivation and the volition to expend further effort. Effort persistence is most important when intended outcomes include the long-term continuation of professional behaviors after graduation.

The MVP model provides a framework for thinking about the ways in which motivation and volition can be developed and enhanced, and it offers opportunities for teacher to incorporate instructional designs that demonstrate the importance of professional values. This helps candidates to build habits of thought and behavior that represent the best in teaching.

At this point, we must acknowledge that with respect to outcomes such as the development of values, attitudes, and commitments, undergraduate curricula in teacher education can only begin to prepare candidates for their future professional lives. Candidates may possess values and motivations that impel them toward teaching careers (Effort direction, MVP Segment 1). They may have these characteristics enhanced by their educational experiences and thus be motivated to engage further with the curriculum and to take action to deepen their learning (Effort initiation, MVP Segment 2). They may have positive experiences and success as a result of their efforts and thus sustain their original motivations leading to the completion of their programs (Effort persistence, MVP Segment 3). However, when graduates enter their professional lives, they may encounter conditions and situations that conflict with their values and expectations, and these conditions can negatively affect all three types of effort, causing frustration and disillusionment. Johnson and Birkeland (2003) investigated teachers' career decisions and they stressed the importance of ongoing professional development and "Integrated Professional Cultures" that "engaged teachers of all experience levels in collegial and collaborative efforts" (2003, 605). They concluded that such school cultures promote success for new teachers, but that, "unless (teachers') experiences are rewarding, they will likely transfer to another school or leave teaching altogether" (2003, 606). In circumstances where the experiences are not rewarding, persistence in adhering to high standards of professional behavior will be more difficult. Professional attitudes and behaviors may be difficult to sustain when there is constant diminishing of the profession itself, but even in the face of these difficult situations, teacher education programs still strive to instill professional values and dispositions in candidates.

Some Instructional Approaches That Relate to Affective Learning

Fortunately, there is a considerable array of literature that relates to instructional design for affective learning, and this literature meshes nicely with the MVP model. For example, the External Inputs noted in the first part of

Segment 1 of the MVP model and the first part of Keller's ARCS model (1987) focus on gaining learners' attention, arousing learners' curiosity, capitalizing on learners' interests and creating or enhancing positive expectancies about performance. Bain's discussion of "What the Best College Teachers Do" (2004) is one of the many works that stress the importance of quickly establishing a classroom climate that encourages reflection, provides an open environment for examination of ideas, and allows experimentation and the development of novel solutions without rigid adherence to the idea that there is only one right answer. The freedom to try new strategies or to approach problems from different or even unique, individual perspectives keeps learners engaged and active. Importantly in this chapter, intrinsic and extrinsic motivation can be embedded in the stimuli and experiences used in instruction and in the contingencies built into the consequences of performance.

As noted earlier in this chapter, cognitive outcomes must be considered along with affective outcomes if instruction is to achieve its maximum effectiveness. Although exploration of candidates' personal beliefs is important and should begin early, activities at the higher end of the affective domain taxonomy (for example, Modification and Categorization in Neuman and Friedman, 2010) require a deeper understanding of the intended outcomes and must come from more complex cognitive activity. When teachers make instructional decisions, they are operating at the highest levels of both the knowledge dimension and the cognitive process dimension described in the revised taxonomy of cognitive objectives (Anderson and Krathwohl 2001). Without this cognitive foundation, understanding the desired professional dispositions and behaviors and developing the will to take action are more difficult.

Rees, Graham, and Theall (2014) tested this domain relationship in a small-sample study involving four sections of an entry-level teacher education course. The focus was on developing better learner understanding of affective outcomes and the professional behaviors those outcomes would suggest. In the fall semester, no unusual instructional strategies were employed, but specific instructional strategies such as knowledge surveys, class discussions, dialogue, and a case study were used in the spring semester. Pre- and posttests required candidates to provide specific types of teacher behaviors that would exemplify successful achievement of the affective outcomes. Significant differences were found between beginning and end-of-semester scores in the spring semester and between fall and spring end-of semester scores. The authors concluded that some basic and well-established instructional strategies had had positive effects, but they also noted that, although the reflection the activities generated was useful, "This reflection will not guarantee actual future behaviors aligned with intended outcomes, especially if working environment pressures mitigate against such behaviors" (2014, 51). In the remainder of this chapter, we present brief descriptions of some useful instructional theories and strategies.

Deep and Surface Approaches. Biggs (1987, 2001) referred to "deep and surface approaches" to learning. "Deep" approaches are characterized by a willingness to engage more completely with content and a desire to acquire useful knowledge. They involve willful action by learners who seek information that allows them to grasp both basic principles and more complex issues. "Surface" approaches center only on acquisition of information sufficient to pass tests or meet other course requirements. These approaches are more extrinsically motivated and although they can lead to some self-regulation and effort (MVP Segment 3), they do not necessarily make best use of mental resources described in MVP Segment 4. Engagement with content will be reduced and more effort put into pure memorization.

Elaboration Likelihood. Elaboration likelihood refers to the extent to which learners engage in cognitive activity and issue-relevant thinking when formulating positions. Petty and Cacioppo (1986) and Cacioppo et al. (1986) studied the relationship of elaboration likelihood to attitude formation and found that individuals who desired more cognition elaborated on issues in determining and developing attitudes. Those who did not desire more cognition did not elaborate on issues when forming attitudes. A second finding was that individuals who elaborated cognitively were more likely to act on the dispositions developed during attitude formation. In other words, the studies can be said to support the notion that "deep" approaches to learning help learners to more fully and carefully develop attitudes based on sophisticated understanding, and those attitudes lead to dispositions that affect future behavior. Motivation and volition are both necessary if attitude formation is a desired outcome, and instructional strategies that require students to engage in elaboration and deep learning can help learners to develop professional attitudes and dispositions.

Knowledge Surveys. One example of an early intervention strategy involves the use of "knowledge surveys" (Nuhfer and Knipp 2003) that serve many purposes including providing baseline data for comparison to later assessments. These instruments assess learners' perceptions of their knowledge and help learners to understand what they do not know (Bell and Volckman 2011; Kruger and Dunning 1999) so that instruction can focus on correcting misconceptions and lack of specific knowledge. As MVP Segment 1 inputs, knowledge surveys can make performance expectancies more realistic and promote effort direction, and they can also influence emotions and promote commitment that can lead to effort initiation. With learners' incremental success, they can support effort persistence, and when used in a posttest mode along with other assessments, they can continue the motivational cycle by providing evidence of success that results in satisfaction in MVP Segment 6.

Discussion, Case Studies, and Reflection. Whenever the intention of instruction is to help learners to make responsible and ethical decisions and to act accordingly, it is important to engage in activities that require articulation and consideration of opinions, beliefs, and alternatives. Many well-established strategies provide opportunities for such activity whether in class or as assigned work, but these strategies are similar in that they follow a common sequence: (1) raise an issue; (2) solicit opinions; (3) seek conflicting or corroborating information; (4) weigh alternatives; (5) reach consensus, or if not, gather more information for further consideration. In class discussion situations, simple prompts such as "What do you think?," "What would you do?," "Why would you do that?," "What else could be done?," or "Do you agree?" can be effective. Student-to-student dialogue in pairs or small groups can be added as the questions and issues get discussed. Outside the classroom, web-based discussion forums in learning management systems accomplish the same purposes, allowing learners to present opinions or post brief journal entries to discussion groups. A recorder in each group can forward consensus opinions to a discussion area for the entire class. Groups can also be assigned roles to argue positions and the teacher can monitor and assess individual or group progress. Perhaps the most tested strategy is the use of case studies (Christensen and Hansen 1987), which can be the basis for exploring ethical and professional issues. These methods cut across all six sections of the MVP model. They provide inputs that arouse curiosity and interest, support persistence, provide assistance with mental resource and time management, and involve deliberation and reflection. They help learners address affective issues by focusing on exploration of individual beliefs and dispositions, and by asking learners to make and justify professional and ethical decisions.

Cooperative Learning. Although the methods noted here involve some cooperation among learners, strategies for cooperative learning that involve specific processes and assigned roles have been shown to be widely effective (Johnson and Johnson 1989). Cooperative learning offers many motivational benefits. (Panitz 1999, 59–67) lists the benefits of cooperative learning as developing attitude, encouraging persistence, enhancing meaning, fostering student–student and student–teacher interactions, involving self-management, engendering competence, and enhancing satisfaction and self-esteem. These are all elements of Keller's ARCS model (1987) as well as the MVP model.

Service Learning. Service learning involves school and community partnerships in which course content is directly connected to projects that support local needs. Teachers design instruction that targets specific outcomes through learners' engagement in activities that apply what is learned in the classroom to real-world situations. Service learning has been used and studied for almost twenty-five years with regular reports of positive results. Prentice, Robinson, and Patton (2012) reported that service learning produced multiple outcomes including increased relevance of instruction, more student–teacher and student–student interaction, greater student commitment, increased confidence, more persistence, and higher retention rates. They stated, "what stands out ... is the understanding that a single semester of service learning produces multiple student outcomes....

Beyond the classroom, student success lies not only in academic gains, but also in personal, social, and civic development" (2012, 26). Service learning touches on all parts of the MVP not only through personal academic achievement but also through having benefited others.

Field Work. In teacher education, as in the health sciences and social work, apprenticeships, supervised placements, field experiences, and other methods are used to support cognitive and affective outcomes and to provide opportunities for learners to make informed career choices. This acknowledges the reality that not all learners will choose careers in the fields that are identical to their initial interests. In professional fields, it is better for curricula to incorporate experiences that expose learners to the professional roles and responsibilities they will face after graduation, even if that exposure means that some learners will lose motivation and choose to change direction.

Conclusions

The MVP model outlines a dynamic sequence of factors, processes, and outcomes that follow a path from motivation to volition to performance to satisfaction. The process is cyclical in the sense that any outcomes—positive or negative—will affect the process itself. Early inclusion of motivational strategies sets the stage for ongoing reflection and deliberation throughout the curriculum. The strategies presented here include opportunities for deep approaches as well as cognitive elaboration, and they follow the "Seven Principles for Good Practice in Undergraduate Education" outlined by Chickering and Gamson (1987). When intended outcomes include affective objectives, learners must have a coherent array of experiences that challenge them to reflect on their beliefs and to weigh alternatives. Application of ideas into real-world situations provides a solid ground for teacher candidates to consider possible responses and examine the results of the choices they make. If this set of experiences aligns with personal beliefs and attitudes, then learners are more likely to take action. Donald Schön's discussion of "The Reflective Practitioner" (1991) is often cited as an appropriate model for candidates aspiring to teaching careers because constant consideration of how to create and examine conditions for successful learning is a necessary professional teaching activity. Such activity requires commitment, self-regulation, and volition: the will to take action as part of teachers' ongoing efforts to improve performance for themselves and their students.

References

Anderson Lorin W., and David Krathwohl. 2001. *A Taxonomy for Learning, Teaching and Assessing: A Revision of Bloom's Taxonomy of Educational Objectives*. New York: Longman.

Angelo Thomas A., and K. Patricia Cross. 1993. *Classroom Assessment Techniques: A Handbook for College Teachers*, 2nd ed. San Francisco: Jossey Bass.

Bain Ken. 2004. *What the Best College Teachers Do*. Cambridge, MA: Harvard University Press.

Bandura Albert. 1977. "Self-Efficacy: Toward a Unifying Theory of Behavioral Change." *Psychological Review* 84(3): 191–215.

Barnes Candice D., and Janet Filer. 2012. "Disposition Development: A Neglected Voice for the Pursuit of Excellence among College Students." *Faculty Focus* (May): 1–2.

Bell Priscilla, and David Volckmann. 2011. "Knowledge Surveys in General Chemistry: Confidence, Overconfidence and Performance." *Journal of Chemical Education* 88: 1468–1476.

Council for the Accreditation of Educator Preparation. 2013. CAEP Accreditation Standards. http://caepnet.org/~/media/Files/caep/standards/caep-2013-accreditation-standards.pdf

Biggs, John B. 1987. *Approaches to Studying and Learning*. Melbourne: Australian Council for Educational Research.

Biggs John B. 2001. "Enhancing Learning: A Matter of Style or Approach?" In *Perspectives on Thinking, Learning, and Cognition*, edited by Robert J. Sternberg and Li-fang Zhang, 73–100. Mahwah, NJ: Lawrence Erlbaum.

Cacioppo John T., Richard E. Petty, Chuan F. Kao, and Regina Rodriguez. 1986. "Central and Peripheral Routes to Persuasion: An Individual Difference Perspective" *Journal of Personality and Social Psychology* 51(5): 1032–1043.

Chickering Arthur W., and Zelda F. Gamson. 1987. "Seven Principles for Good Practice in Undergraduate Education." *Wingspread Journal* 9(2).

Christensen Carl R., and Abby J. Hansen. 1987. *Teaching and the Case Method*. Cambridge, MA: Harvard Business School.

Duplass James A., and Barbara C. Cruz. 2010. "Professional Dispositions: What's a Social Studies Education Professor to Do?" *Social Studies* 101: 140–151.

Holland, John L. 1997. *Making Vocational Choices*, 3rd ed. Englewood Cliffs, NJ: Prentice-Hall.

Hladkyj Steve, Jason R. Taylor, Sarah T. Pelletier, and Raymond P. Perry. 1999, April 21. "Narrative Emplotment: Meaning and Value in Unpredictable Experience and its Role in Student Motivation." Paper presented at the 80th annual meeting of the American Educational Research Association. Montreal, Canada.

Johnson Roger T., and David W. Johnson. 1989. *Cooperation and Competition Theory and Research*. Edina, MN: Interaction Book Co.

Johnson Susan M., and Sarah E. Birkeland. 2003. "Pursuing a 'Sense of Success': New Teachers Explain their Career Decisions." *American Educational Research Journal* 40 (3): 581–617.

Keller, John M. 1983. "Motivational Design of Instruction." In *Instructional Design Theories and Models: An Overview of Their Current Status*, edited by Charles M. Reigeluth, 386–434. Hillsdale, NJ: Lawrence Erlbaum.

Keller, John M. 1987. "Development and Use of the ARCS Model of Instructional Design." *Journal of Instructional Development* 10(3), 2–10.

Keller, John M. 2008. "An Integrative Theory of Motivation, Volition, and Performance." *Technical Instruction, Cognition, and Learning* 6(2): 79–104.

Kolb, David L. 1984. *Experiential Learning: Experience as the Source of Learning and Development*. Englewood Cliffs, NJ: Prentice Hall.

Krathwohl, David R., Benjamin S. Bloom, and Bertram B. Masia. 1964. *Taxonomy of Educational Objectives. The Classification of Educational Goals. Handbook II: Affective Domain*. New York: David McKay.

Kruger Justin, and David Dunning. 1999. "Unskilled and Unaware of It: How Difficulties in Recognizing One's Own Incompetence Lead to Inflated Self-assessments." *Journal of Personality and Social Psychology* 77(6): 1121–1134.

Menec Vera H., Raymond P. Perry, C. Ward Struthers, Dieter, J. Schonwetter, Frank J. Hechter, and Brila L. Eichholz. 1994. "Assisting At-Risk College Students with Attributional Retraining and Effective Teaching." *Journal of Applied Social Psychology* 24: 675–701.

National Council on Accreditation of Teacher Education. 2008. *NCATE Unit Standards*. http://www.ncate.org/Standards/NCATEUnitStandards/UnitStandardsinEffect2008/tabid/476/Default.aspx#stnd1

Neuman Karen A., and Bruce D. Friedman. 2008, October. "The Art of Effectively Facilitating Professional Socialization in Students Through Affective Learning." Paper presented at the Annual Program Meeting of the Council on Social Work Education, Philadelphia.

Neuman Karen A., and Bruce D. Friedman. 2010. "Affective Learning: A Taxonomy for Teaching Social Work." *Journal of Social Work Values and Ethics* 7(2): 1–12

Nuhfer Edward, and Dolores Knipp. 2003. "The Knowledge Survey: A Tool for All Reasons." In *To Improve the Academy*. Vol. 21, edited by Catherine Wehlburg and Sandra Chadwick-Blossey, 59–78. Bolton, MA: Anker Publications.

Panitz Theodore. 1999. "The Motivational Benefits of Cooperative Learning." *In Motivation from Within: Encouraging Faculty and Students to Excel. New Directions for Teaching and Learning, no.78,* edited by Michael Theall, 59–67. San Francisco: Jossey Bass.

Perry Raymond P., and Jamie L. Magnusson. 1989. Causal Attributions and Perceived Performance: Consequences for College Students' Achievement and Perceived Control in Different Instructional Conditions. *Journal of Educational Psychology* 81: 164–172.

Petty Richard E., and John T. Cacioppo. 1986. *Communication and Persuasion: Central and Peripheral Routes to Attitude Change*. New York: Springer-Verlag.

Piaget, Jean. 1952. *The Origins of Intelligence in Children*. New York: International Universities Press.

Pintrich, Paul R., ed. 1995. *Understanding Self-regulated Learning*. New Directions for Teaching and Learning, no. 63. San Francisco: Jossey Bass.

Prentice Mary, Gail Robinson, and Madeline Patton. 2012. *Cultivating Community Beyond the Classroom*. Washington, DC: American Association of Community Colleges. http://www.aacc.nche.edu/Resources/aaccprograms/horizons/Documents/Cultivating Communities_Aug2012.pdf

Rees Regina M., DeBorah D. Graham, and Michael Theall. 2014. "Helping Teacher Education Candidates to Understand, Accept, and Adopt Professional Dispositions and Behaviors." Ohio Journal of Teacher Education (2): 46–52.

Ricoeur, Paul. 1992. *Oneself as Another*. Chicago: University of Chicago Press.

Rokeach, Milton A. 1960. *The Open and Closed Mind*. New York, NY: Basic Books.

Schön, Donald A. 1991. *Educating the Reflective Practitioner.* San Francisco: Jossey Bass.

Seligman, Martin E. P. 1972. "Learned Helplessness." *Annual Review of Medicine* 23(1): 407–412.

Smart John C., and Kenneth A. Feldman. 1998. "Accentuation Effects of Dissimilar Academic Departments: An Application and Exploration of Holland's Theory." *Research in Higher Education* 39(4): 385–418.

Svinicki, Marilla D. 2004. *Learning and Motivation in the Postsecondary Classroom*. Bolton, MA: Anker.

Theall, Michael, ed. 1999. *Motivation from Within: Encouraging Faculty and Students to Excel*. New Directions for Teaching and Learning, no. 78. San Francisco: Jossey Bass.

Weiner, Bernard. 1974. *Achievement Motivation and Attribution Theory*. Morristown, NJ: General Learning Press.

Zull, James E. 2002. *The Art of Changing the Brain*. Sterling, VA: Stylus.
Zull, James E. 2011. *From Brain to Mind*. Sterling, VA: Stylus.

MICHAEL THEALL is emeritus professor of teacher education, Youngstown State University.

DEBORAH D. GRAHAM is assistant professor of teacher education at Youngstown State University.

5

This chapter describes a Reading and Study Skills program and course that are offered to first-year students who are underprepared or reluctant and who may be at risk for failure in other courses as well as at risk for long-term retention and graduation. The course is discussed with respect to its parallels to the MVP model, and initial evidence of its success is provided. The MVP cycle is reflected in course design and process and in a textbook created specifically to accompany the course.

MVP and College Success for First-Year Students

Karen A. Becker

Reluctant learners—be they "developmental," "at risk," or "underresourced," to name just a few labels—react well to learning environments in which they are not treated in ways that reflect these labels. Fearing being perceived as "not good enough" or "lacking," such students actually blossom and thrive when supplied with not only the "what" and the "how" but also the "why" in their learning environments. Motivation is crucial in this process, as are techniques that promote learners' taking responsibility for their own actions and efforts. Because volitional action such as self-regulation and sustained effort follows this assumption of responsibility, effective instruction for these learners must incorporate a planned sequence of events and experiences that capture interest and prompt action. Providing opportunities for incremental growth and success and outcome contingencies that emphasize goal achievement also promotes sustained effort and perseverance. Thus, helping students to concretely identify and refine their own learning preferences, aptitudes, confidence, locus of control, and self-regulation and helping them to learn other "soft skills" have proven to have long-term effects that promote retention and continued success.

Related Literature

Classes that include reluctant students may have many who come from underresourced backgrounds or circumstances such as those described by Becker, Krodel, and Tucker (2009). In these cases, their lives are filled with many obstacles, including a mind-set that may not prioritize their education over daily interferences such as a broken-down car or a family member in need of attention. Relationships override achievement in the worlds of many underresourced students. Thus, starting in Segments 1–3 of the motivation–volition–performance (MVP) model (Keller, Chapter 1 in this issue), it becomes crucial to facilitate actionable interest and curiosity. This provides reasons for making school a priority and for initiating the effort and self-regulation that lead to success. These are not simple tasks for teachers or learners and they require constant attention to learners' progress, reactions, emotions, and attitudes. One of the obstacles to self-regulation is the underresourced student's inexperience with grasping abstract concepts. Learners often overestimate the extent of their knowledge and understanding (Kruger and Dunning 1999). The more abstract the concepts to be learned, the more difficult it is for many learners to grasp the true extent of their knowledge. This is especially so for underprepared learners.

Students' beliefs about knowledge, learning, and ability are very important. Paulsen and Feldman (1999) examined six motivational constructs with respect to four dimensions of beliefs. They considered intrinsic and extrinsic motivation, task value, control of learning, self-efficacy, and test anxiety and correlated these constructs with beliefs about knowledge. Students were asked whether knowledge is simple (as in learning facts) or complex (as in developing deeper understanding) and whether it is certain (as in absolute) or uncertain (as in evolving). They were also asked whether learning is a quick or slow process and whether ability is fixed or changeable. The correlations Paulsen and Feldman reported indicated that students with naïve beliefs (that is, that knowledge is simple, certain, and quickly learned) and those who believed that ability is fixed were more extrinsically motivated, had more test anxiety, valued academic tasks less, had less perceived control of learning, and had lower self-efficacy. Clearly, this group of mind-sets is not productive in terms of academic achievement. These results emphasize two things: (1) the predispositions of students in these courses to have lower expectancies and more external locus of control and (2) the value of the kind of training provided in the course described here. Training that helps students to understand and accept that they can influence outcomes and can achieve their goals can make a big difference. Menec et al. (1994) demonstrated that "attributional retraining" had a positive effect on at-risk students' attitudes, motivation, expectancies, and performance. From a motivational and volitional perspective, this training can enhance the kinds of effort shown in MVP Segments 1, 2, and 3 and can positively influence emotional and rational processing of outcomes (in Segment 6) that will result in satisfaction and sustained effort. As Zull stresses (2002, 221–244), there is great power in being able to say "We did this ourselves." However, students must believe that such an outcome is possible. Focus on long-term success through incremental goal setting and goal achievement; the development of reading, test-taking, and related skills; and continuous reflection on motivation, effort, and performance supports the gradual acquisition of these beliefs and the benefits that come with it.

Positive expectancies for success can be sabotaged not only by previous negative experiences but also by the continued barrage of external obstacles and interferences such as lack of knowledge about higher education because of being first-generation students and value systems that do not recognize a diploma as a beginning but simply as an end point.

Discussions of courses and activities included in "freshman year experience" programs (for example, Upcraft and Gardner 2001; Stumpf and Hunt 1993) support the conclusion that skill development is important, and suggestions for evaluating such first-year programs (Gardner, Barefoot, and Swing 2001) emphasize exploring if and how the combination of traditional academic and soft skills has been developed.

The trick, of course, is that reluctant learners need well-designed instruction in order to establish motivational and volitional habits that take them through the six segments of the MVP model. Further, as the model demonstrates, the instruction is best delivered by someone who is also motivated to dig deeply into the many factors that affect teaching and learning and to create curriculum in which students discover and elaborate on new ideas and develop their own skills and aptitudes while they learn content. The links between learner aptitudes and instructional treatments have been known for some time (Cronbach and Snow 1967) and the more a teacher can develop instruction that capitalizes on learner strengths and leads to new skill development, the more learners will benefit.

Reading and Study Skills (RSS) 1510: A Kind of Reverse Psychology

The reading and study skills courses that I have been supervising and teaching for over 20 years are about metalearning—learning about learning. Teaching these classes certainly implies a two-way street: students interested in learning and instructors who can facilitate that process. Segments 1–3 of the MVP model are important in the first moments and hours of class time, and a sort of "reverse psychology" is employed in class discussions to convince reluctant students that they have what it takes to be successful. Usually, we think of reverse psychology as challenging someone by suggesting that he or she cannot achieve a goal. Because reluctant students already fear such an outcome, that approach is risky at best and particularly dangerous if students exhibit any tendency toward "learned helplessness" (Seligman 1972). The "reverse" here is more related to altering the direction of students' expectancies by showing them that they can learn effective academic strategies and succeed in their courses. Put differently, the reverse challenge can be stated as "You *can* do what you don't think you can do." We achieve this by helping learners to uncover and refine the skills needed for the various tasks that lie ahead in their college lives and careers.

Immediately uncovering and cultivating positive emotions and intentions supports what might have been a hidden interest or curiosity that is often viewed as "too cool for school" by students placed in developmental coursework. Because students sometimes walk into these courses feeling punished, it is important to establish a positive environment that includes instruction about not only what the students should be doing and suggestions about how they might do it but also about the theories and science behind these "shoulds" and "mights." This leads us to the fourth and fifth MVP segments that focus on engagement, metacognition, and the mental activities associated with effective learning. Again, in RSS 1510, emphasis is on skill development as an enabling objective that will lead to achievement of overall course goals.

Learners are exposed to and are required to practice techniques for note-taking, memory development, test-taking, and extracting important information from sources (for example, from texts, lectures, course syllabi, and importantly, from teachers via dialogue and questioning). Reluctant learners are not used to thinking of teachers as people they can talk to about their learning. This perceived distance can be a significant deterrent. Many well-established guides have stressed student–teacher interaction and other socialization activities as critical to success. Chickering and Gamson (1987) include interaction with faculty and peers as one of the "Seven Principles for Effective Practice in Undergraduate Education." Kuh and others (2010) incorporate collaboration and interaction into the set of Engagement Indicators that are reported in the National Survey of Student Engagement. Pascarella (1985) stated that socialization was a key to affective development. Pascarella and Terenzini (1991, 2005) reviewed three decades of research on the effects of college and found socialization to be a key element. Beyond this work, Loes, Pascarella, and Umbach (2012) reported that complex thinking was prompted by being challenged to consider new ideas and points of view that arise when diversity is present in curricula and courses.

Perhaps most important with respect to RSS 1510 were studies that demonstrated the importance of effective instruction. Pascarella, Salisbury, and Blaich (2011) found that effective instruction was a primary determinant of college persistence. Loes and Pascarella (2015) reported that learner perceptions of teacher clarity and organization were associated with gains in critical thinking, persistence, academic motivation, and student use of deep approaches to learning. This work reflects two other important areas of study. Feldman (1989) found that the six-teacher behaviors most correlated with student achievement were (1) organization, (2) clarity, (3) perceived outcome, (4) stimulating interest in content, (5) encouragement and openness, and (6) availability and helpfulness. These elements are woven throughout the RSS 1510 course design. Biggs (1987) stressed that learners who use "deep approaches" (that is, seeking to elaborate on new information to develop better understanding) perform better than those who use only "surface" approaches (that is, seeking to learn only what seems

Figure 5.1. Information Processing Model

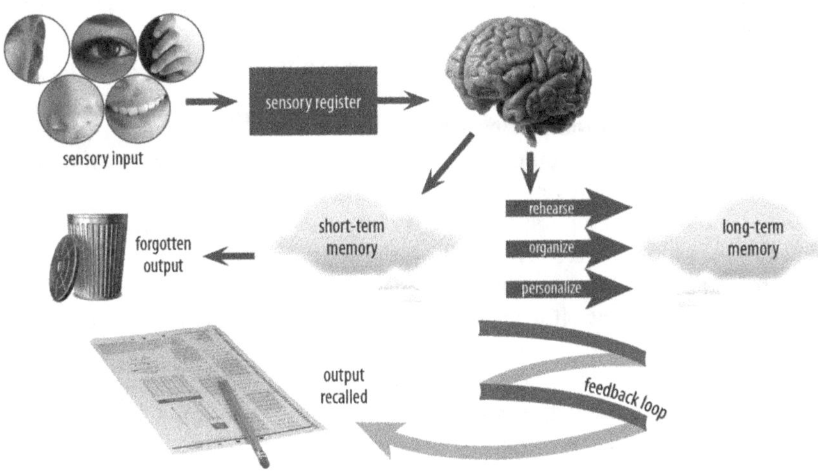

to be required for a grade). In RSS 1510, these ideas are reviewed and students develop skills that support deep approaches. For example, emphasis on techniques for improving memory includes organizing materials, setting incremental goals, monitoring progress, self-testing, and regular reflection on materials.

A Text to Accompany the Course. Several years ago, the instructors of reading and study skills classes joined forces to create our own textbook. Now in its fourth edition (Becker and Towler 2015), this text takes a what, why, and how approach to introducing topics. In this way, students are given more than a menu of strategies (what) and steps for doing so (how) but also some general theories about why these strategies are necessary and work. The textbook is organized to start with some theory but eventually connects the theoretical information with specific learning strategies, and all the parts of the Attention, Relevance, Confidence, and Satisfaction (ARCS) model (Keller 1987) and the MVP model are reflected along the way. At the outset, students are introduced to an information processing model as a foundation for understanding different learning preferences.

The "art" of learning includes the student's soft skills such as self-management/time management (MVP Segments 3 and 4) and self-regulation of body, mind, and emotions (MVP Segment 4). In many ways, these soft skills are often undeveloped in at-risk or underresourced students. However, when students understand the connections to learning and performance (MVP Segment 5), they often become motivated to investigate further. Another focus includes envisioning a process of transitioning from novice to expert. This focus identifies key steps in learning and promotes greater satisfaction with accomplishments along the learning process. Learning that there are many types of individual differences, for example, information input preferences, learning styles (Grasha 1996) and types of intelligence (Gardner 1993), students begin to recognize their own "art" and they see the "science" behind it. Exploring these topics generates interest and curiosity and demonstrates relevance because the subjects of exploration are the learners themselves. As these topics converge in their minds, a majority of the students begin to see that they do have the potential to learn, their expectancies become more positive, and locus of control (Weiner 1986) becomes more internal. This also links to MVP Segment 1. From the instructors' perspective, it is important to specify the objectives that enable students to move through the model. This process is similar to moving from novice to expert recursively and it reinforces the notion that learning is not purely linear. Teachers can demonstrate how getting new information and reflecting on its "fit" with existing beliefs can lead to developing new ideas. The process is clearly consistent with the alignment of domains and knowledge in the revised Bloom taxonomy (Anderson and Krathwohl 2001; Bloom, Englehart, Furst, Hill, and Krathwohl 1956), and given the emphasis in RSS 1510 on metacognition, students are led to higher levels of thinking in a novice-to-expert sequence. The intent is not to make beginning or reluctant students experts in one semester but rather to work with them through a process that allows them to better understand the kind of learning they will be doing.

Once motivated by the information that actually demonstrates to them that they have potential, students are more confident—as in Segment 1 of the MVP model and Confidence in the ARCS model—and ready to move on to evaluating their priorities, values, and the barriers that might hold them back. As this process evolves, students begin to identify what motivates them to be in college and to seek the degrees and majors that are more aligned with their interests and preferences. Many students go to college "because they are supposed to," and the discussion of their interests and motivations begins to demonstrate the transition from extrinsic to intrinsic motivation. As they come to grips with these underlying mind-sets, students are encouraged to take control of their "BME"—body, mind, and emotions. Touching here on both Segment 1 and Segment 6 of Keller's Model, students are reminded not only that their roles in the learning process do not stop at the consumption of knowledge but also that they must be aware of their own situations and continuously do things—such as getting enough sleep, managing their time, trying to avoid stressful situations, and finding a suitable place to study—that can improve their learning. Grounding this BME awareness in new knowledge about the science of brain function described by Todd Zakrajsek in Chapter 2 of this issue, students can take one more step to understanding the levels of knowing necessary to college learning. Then, as students actually go through an introduction to the revised taxonomy (Anderson and Krathwohl 2001), they develop the ability to analyze the academic work they must do so that they can plan effective ways of managing their effort and their learning.

Table 5.1. Hook, Book, Look, and Took" Sequence

Components of Tutor Session Planner	*Explanation*	*MVP Model Segment*
HOOK	Getting connected to the concept. Tutor asks what students already know about the concept.	Segment 1 Effort direction Segment 2 Effort initiation Segment 3 Effort persistence
BOOK	Understand the concept. Tutor and students review information in the text and elsewhere.	Segment 3 Effort persistence Segment 4 Monitoring and cognition Segment 5 Learning and performance
LOOK	Construct meaning through application. Students practice concepts with tutor's assistance and modeling.	Segment 5 Learning and performance
TOOK	Set a takeaway goal to practice/use the concept. Student set goals for how to use concepts during the week.	Segment 6 Consequences with a return to Segment 2 Effort initiation

The Secret Fairy Dust. The use of weekly learning communities is a significant factor for this movement from information processing to motivation and volition. Small groups of students meet with trained peer tutors who are sophomores and above with 3.0 grade-point averages who have passed the course or were not required to take it. They are paid to meet weekly to review course material and engage students in experimentation and reflection on the strategies and theories presented in the textbook and discussed in face-to-face class time. The tutors provide real-life feedback about how students might adopt and adapt the strategies they are learning, and this takes place in the low-threat environment of small groups. Each week, peer tutors ask the students to write a goal for the tutoring session and/or for the week. Goal setting provides a critical link to Segments 2 and 3 in the MVP model because self-regulation (Pintrich 1995) requires a target goal, and planning the actions that lead to that goal promotes volitional behavior. Tutors follow session planners designed by the instructor to engage students in using new learning strategies. In this way, students are motivated and prompted by people just like themselves who monitor and focus their attention on a task they might not have otherwise conceived of or attempted. Each session planner includes a full-spectrum reflection of the MVP model. We call this the "hook, book, look, and took" sequence.

Discussions in the tutoring sessions might include comments from the peer tutors such as, "I tried this in my _____ class and it was really helpful, but I might not have used it in other classes" and "I know this looks like a lot of work, but it takes effort to really learn in some of your classes, especially when you get into upper division." Course instructors are in the classroom with tutors and the student groups, and so, can answer questions, provide explanations, clarify issues, or point out common ideas or themes that arise from group discussions.

Wishful Thinking versus Fear of Failure. Week after week, students are asked to reflect on how they applied the learning from previous weeks (or not) in this and their other classes. For instance, students are prompted to select tasks that they think might help them improve their organization of time and materials, or they may identify a learning strategy to employ in reading their textbooks and online materials as they prepare for a test. When goals are analyzed, comments from tutors integrate the emotional component of learning with the cognitive piece. That is, tutors' comments and personal experiences can encourage students and demonstrate that the techniques can work. Tutors are trained, of course, to find the positive side of the learning situations, even when things aren't going well—a sort of cup half-filled attitude that says, "Well, that didn't work perfectly. What could you try instead?"

The tutors act as "reflection coaches" who launch the feedback loop in Keller's model. They do so along with students by examining what happened, why it happened, and who is responsible. This draws attention to the importance of having an internal locus of control, attributing outcomes to appropriate causes, and also having positive expectancies about success. Thus, when students struggle with new concepts, they become aware of their own roles in the process. This awareness keeps them moving through the MVP model in a way that brings about a layering of analysis, application, and eventually, satisfaction and completion. The relationship of support and motivation creates an environment for use of the entire MVP model.

Graduation and Retention Data

Although there has not been a formal data gathering process over the full span of RSS programs and courses, recent data have been collected and analyzed. These data concern students who were enrolled in RSS 1510 in the 2008–2009 academic year. Retention and graduation data for these students were compared to institutional, state, and national groups to provide at least a partial picture of the impact and effectiveness of RSS 1510.

Graduation rates were calculated by identifying a group of first-time, full-time degree/certificate seeking undergraduate students and tracking their degree completion status over a six-year period. Six years is the maximum time expected for completing baccalaureate degree requirements. For reporting purposes, typical graduation rates are calculated at the conclusion of the fourth, fifth, and sixth years. According to the data, the students who took the RSS 1510 in Fall 2008 through Fall 2009 are graduating at a rate of 30%. This figure is higher than the recorded rate of the institution, the state comparison group, and the national comparison group. The range of comparison group percentages was from 14 to 30%.

Retention rates were measured from the fall of first enrollment to the following fall. From Fall 2008 through Fall 2009, students taking the Reading and Study Skills courses ranked second highest among the groups, exceeding institutional and national, but not state averages. These retention rates come from students that are enrolled fulltime or at least for twelve credit hours per semester. Retention rates were similar across groups with only five percentage points separating the top and bottom groups.

Only one cohort of RSS students (those enrolled in 2008–2009) was involved and no inferential statistical tests were applied, so firm conclusions cannot be drawn, but the results nonetheless suggest success for the RSS courses, especially with respect to graduation rates. These data also suggest the potential value of a more complete investigation of the extent to which RSS courses effectively deal with "reluctant" students, promote academic achievement and persistence in pursuit of long-term academic goals, and provide useful information for planning other first-year programs and influencing the design of disciplinary courses.

Conclusions

Literature dealing with higher education teaching and learning provides strong support for programs such as Reading and Study Skills and also provides evidence that including motivational and volitional factors in course design supports improved persistence and performance, especially among reluctant learners. The MVP model is clearly reflected in RSS 1510 course design and in everyday classroom process. The model is reflected from initiation of interest and curiosity at the start of the courses (MVP Segment 1), through building confidence and positive expectancies via incremental achievements (MVP Segment 1), through development of volitional and self-regulatory habits (MVP Segments 2 and 3), through metacognitive practice analyzing learning situations and the application of new learning skills (MVP Segments 4 and 5), to reflection about performance and consequences (MVP Segment 6). The feedback loop from Segment 6 to Segments 1, 2, and 3 allows two positive results: (1) when self-set goals are achieved and satisfaction is felt and effort will be sustained; and (2) even if goals are not fully achieved or there is occasional failure, RSS 1510 course process provides mechanisms for understanding and processing these results in a productive way that supports persistence. This positive motivational cycle is important for all learners but particularly for beginning students, reluctant students, and those whose past academic experiences have not been successful.

References

Anderson, Lorin W., and David Krathwohl. 2001. *A Taxonomy for Learning, Teaching and Assessing: A Revision of Bloom's Taxonomy of Educational Objectives*. New York: Longman.

Becker, Karen A., and Kerry Towler. 2015. *The Art and Science of Quality Learning*, 4th ed. Cincinnati, OH: Van-Griner Publishing.

Becker, Karen A., Karla Krodel, and Bethany Tucker. 2009. *Understanding and Engaging Under-resourced College Students*. Highlands, TX: aha! Process.

Biggs, John. 1987. *Student Approaches to Learning and Studying*. Melbourne: Australian Council for Educational Research.

Bloom, Benjamin S., Max D. Englehart, Edward J. Furst, Walter H. Hill, and David R. Krathwohl. 1956. *Taxonomy of Educational Objectives. The Classification of Educational Goals. Handbook I: Cognitive Domain*. New York: David McKay.

Chickering, Arthur W., and Zelda F. Gamson. 1987. "Seven Principles for Good Practice in Undergraduate Education." *Wingspread Journal* 9(2).

Cronbach, Lee J., and Richard E. Snow. 1967. *Individual Differences in Learning Ability as a Function of Instructional Variables. Final Report*. Washington, DC: U.S. Department of Health, Education, and Welfare, Office of Education.

Feldman, Kenneth A. 1989. "The Association Between Student Ratings of Specific Instructional Dimensions and Student Achievement: Refining and Extending the Synthesis of Data from Multi-section Validity Studies." *Research in Higher Education* 30(4): 583–645.

Gardner, Howard.1993. *Frames of Mind: The Theory of Multiple Intelligences*. New York: Basic Books.

Gardner, John N., Betsy O. Barefoot, and Randy L. Swing. 2001. *Guidelines for Evaluating the First-Year Experience at Four-Year Colleges*, 2nd ed. Columbia, SC: University of South Carolina, National Resource Center for the First-Year Experience® and Students in Transition.

Grasha, Anthony F. 1996. *Teaching with Style*. Pittsburgh, PA: Alliance Press.

Keller, John M. 1987. "Development and Use of the ARCS Model of Instructional Design." *Journal of Instructional Development* 10(3): 2–10.

Kruger, Justin, and David Dunning. 1999. "Unskilled and Unaware of It: How Difficulties in Recognizing One's Own Incompetence Lead to Inflated Self-assessments." *Journal of Personality and Social Psychology* 77(6): 1121–1134.

Kuh, George D., Jillian Kinzie, John H. Schuh, Elizabeth J. Whitt, and Associates. 2010. *Student Success in College: Creating Conditions that Matter*. San Francisco: Jossey-Bass.

Loes, Chad N., and Ernest T. Pascarella. 2015. "The Benefits of Good Teaching Extend Beyond Course Achievement." *Journal of the Scholarship of Teaching and Learning* 15(2): 1–13.

Loes, Chad N., Ernest T. Pascarella, and Paul D. Umbach. 2012. "Effects of Diversity Experiences on Critical Thinking Skills: Who Benefits?" *Journal of Higher Education* 83(1): 1–25.

Menec, Vera H., Raymond P. Perry, C. Ward Struthers, Dieter J. Schonwetter, Frank J. Hechter, and Brila L. Eichholz. 1994. "Assisting At-Risk College Students with Attributional Retraining and Effective Teaching." *Journal of Applied Social Psychology* 24: 675–701.

Pascarella, Ernest T. 1985. "Students' Affective Development Within the College Environment." *Journal of Higher Education* 56(6): 640–663.

Pascarella, Ernest T., Marc H. Salisbury, and Charles Blaich. 2011. "Exposure to Effective Instruction and College Student Persistence: A Multi-institutional Replication and Extension." *Journal of College Student Development* 52(1): 4–19.

Pascarella, Ernest T., and Patrick T. Terenzini. 1991. *How College Affects Students*. San Francisco: Jossey Bass.
Pascarella, Ernest T., and Patrick T. Terenzini. 2005. *How College Affects Students. Vol. 2: A Third Decade of Research*. San Francisco: Jossey Bass
Paulsen, Michael B., and Kenneth A. Feldman. 1999. "Student Motivation and Epistemological Beliefs." In *Motivation from Within: Approaches for Encouraging Faculty and Students to Excel*. New Directions for Teaching and Learning, no. 78, edited by Michael Theall, 17–26. San Francisco: Jossey Bass.
Pintrich, Paul R., ed. 1995. *Understanding Self-Regulated Learning*. New Directions for Teaching and Learning, no. 63. San Francisco: Jossey Bass.
Seligman, Martin E. P. 1972. "Learned Helplessness." *Annual Review of Medicine* 23(1): 407–412.
Stumpf, Gerry, and Pat Hunt. 1993. "The Effect of an Orientation Course on Retention and Academic Standing on Entering Freshmen, Controlling for the Volunteer Effect." *Journal of the Freshman Year Experience* 5(1): 7–17.
Upcraft, M. Lee, John N. Gardner, and Associates. 2001. *The Freshman Year Experience: Helping Students to Survive and Succeed in College*. San Francisco: Jossey Bass.
Vroom, Victor H. 1964. *Work and Motivation*. New York: McGraw-Hill.
Weiner, Bernard. 1986. *An Attributional Theory of Motivation and Emotion*. New York: Springer-Verlag.
Wlodkowski, Raymond J., and Margery E. Ginsberg. 1995. *Diversity and Motivation: Culturally Responsive Teaching*. San Francisco: Jossey Bass.
Zull, James E. 2002. *The Art of Changing the Brain*. Sterling, VA: Stylus Publishing.

KAREN A. BECKER is coordinator of the Reading and Study Skills Center at Youngstown State University.

6

As faculty and faculty developers, we sometimes forget that the principles of learning and motivation that we apply to students also apply to us. This chapter illustrates how the MVP model can be used to create effective faculty development activities.

From Keller's MVP Model to Faculty Development Practice

Marilla D. Svinicki

Faculty development began to flourish in the early 1970s and focused on programs to support the motivation of faculty not long after that. It is informative to look back at what some of the theorists and practitioners were saying then and see what progress has been made. One of the early papers on motivating faculty for teaching was written by James Bess (1977). In this analysis of the rewards for teaching, Bess laid out a list of possible sources of the lack of motivation for teaching at the postsecondary level. I paraphrase them here.

- The aims of education are hard to specify and this makes the outcomes of teaching difficult to determine, so measuring learning and change is also difficult.
- There are ambiguous and conflicting demands on instructors.
- There is not much variation in the routine of teaching the same course repeatedly so it's hard to stay motivated.
- Teaching and learning are very complex activities so there is a lot to know about being an effective teacher.
- As the situation changes, being aware of one's own teaching becomes more difficult.

When we compare this list of challenges with Keller's (2010) motivation–volition–performance (MVP) model as updated in Chapter 1 of this issue, we can see that the same challenges can affect faculty motivation. Although Bess was focused on motivation for teaching and Keller's model is not restricted to any one area of faculty life, we can make connections between the model and the types of faculty development programs that have grown up from those early discussions of faculty development.

NEW DIRECTIONS FOR TEACHING AND LEARNING, no. 152, Winter 2017 © 2017 Wiley Periodicals, Inc.
Published online in Wiley Online Library (wileyonlinelibrary.com) • DOI: 10.1002/tl.20270

The purpose of this chapter is to look at the MVP model applied to faculty development from a practice perspective, tying practices to the model, and considering how that model may point out blanks in practice that could be considered for future programs.

The MVP Model

Motivation may be one of the most important, but also most fragmented, areas of theory, research, and practice in psychology since psychology moved toward being more scientific and evidence based in the middle of the twentieth century. The difficulty of studying it is compounded by the fact that there are so many microprocess models from so many theorists, many with different names for the same phenomenon or the same names for different phenomena. Fenstermacher and Richardson (1994) claim this is a healthy confusion that forces writers to either integrate or isolate their version of motivation theory in or from the rest of the theories. Attempting to integrate motivation theories can be done but sometimes creates more confusion than integration. The model presented in Chapter 1 has a very solid theory and research base and much promise. Nevertheless, it is so inclusive that it makes even seasoned experts stop and think about what is proposed before moving forward in practice. The novice may be amazed and inspired by the skeletal model highlighted in this issue but will soon find that much rich detail hides behind each component, and each box in the model is only skimming the surface. It is possible that someone not already familiar with all the motivation subtheories might find it difficult to move forward without a lot more information or help from someone in the field. Perhaps this issue of New Directions will help in that quest.

Relating Practice to Theory

In recognition of the richness of the MVP model, I am choosing to provide examples from existing faculty development practices that represent applications of its various components. In doing this, I am not suggesting that the practitioners who initiated each practice were doing so to conform to a theoretically based aspect of motivation. Practices can be successful whether or not we derive them from a theory. However, as practitioners become more familiar with the MVP model, they might be able to detect gaps in using the model in designing programs. This could lead to new practices or modifications of old practices to enhance an ongoing faculty development program. Even more desirable would be to have the gaps reported back to the theorists in hopes of making the model even more complete. I will leave that comprehensive analysis of the model to a future researcher and confine this chapter to showing how concrete practices relate to the theory. I have also chosen to omit a discussion of the activities that constitute Segment 5 of the model because it focuses on learning and a full discussion of that topic would exceed my mandate for this chapter.

MVP Segment 1. Motivational influences are "external inputs" of the environment that spark the motivation of the faculty member to engage in new learning or teaching experiences. In the "Psychological environment" part of the model, Keller lists curiosity, values, and expectancies. I look at how taking each of those components into consideration could enhance the probability that a faculty member would engage in a development program.

Curiosity. Certainly an advanced scholar in any field is curious. When some puzzle arises in her own disciplinary or practice area, she is motivated to find out why that happened and she will expend effort to understand it. The same could be true for any component of her faculty responsibilities, but a lot of faculty development tends to focus on teaching. So, if the faculty development program at this faculty member's institution could design a program around an instructional puzzle, it would be providing an external stimulus to draw faculty in by tapping faculty curiosity.

An early example of this kind of programming was the Harvard Assessment Seminars (Light 1990). Light wanted to get Harvard's faculty interested in answering their own questions about students' learning behaviors. He convened a group of interested faculty to decide which aspects of their students' behavior they were curious about. The group generated its own questions, ones that were sparked by their experiences with Harvard students. With that as a starting point, the group formed a research team to gather data and to use what they found to design instructional interventions to help the students get more out of their classes.

One could argue that this External inputs section of the MVP is about external factors whereas curiosity is more of an internal factor. The issue of what constitutes "intrinsic" versus "extrinsic" sources of motivation has been debated for a long time. Bess (1997) discussed this difficulty as one of the ongoing questions in motivating faculty and in a concluding chapter of his book, Bess maintained that although faculty motivation can be self-driven, it is also influenced by local context and the overall context of higher education. More important is the idea that although each of these contexts exercises some control, they constantly interact to influence both intrinsic and extrinsic motivation. This interpretation of the sources of motivation is supported by research by Blackburn and colleagues (Blackburn, Bieber, et al. 1991; Blackburn, Lawrence, et al. 1991). In a large study looking at variables related to motivation and high performance, they found that self-evaluations as competent (intrinsic) and perceptions of institutional support for their work (extrinsic) were the best predictors of faculty productivity and satisfaction.

A more recent theory that attempts to reconcile the concepts of intrinsic and extrinsic motivation is self-determination theory by Deci and Ryan (2000) and the concept of internalization (Ryan and Deci 2000). They proposed that through the process of internalization, things that start out as extrinsically motivating—that is, under the control of an outside source—become integrated into the personal control structure of the individual such that they begin to appear intrinsically motivating—that is, under the control of the individual. In reality, a mixture of outside causes and internal causes actually controls most behaviors. The importance of faculty developers recognizing what might be considered an intrinsic motivation factor and therefore beyond their control is that it gives designers greater understanding of the instructor's thinking so that they can create a more attractive and interesting extrinsic environment in which to work: one that supports existing intrinsic motivators in the faculty member.

An early lesson learned by faculty developers was that programs designed around faculty curiosity and questions would always be more motivating than an externally chosen topic, an idea related self-determination theory (Ryan and Deci 2000). The crux of this theory is the fulfillment of three basic individual needs: feeling competent (efficacy), feeling in control of one's situation (autonomy), and feeling part of a supportive social group (relatedness). These three needs, when fulfilled, strengthen the individual's motivation to take on new challenges over their own situations.

Recent examples of this concept of drawing faculty together around a topic that appeals to their curiosity would be the growth of learning communities (Richlin and Cox 2004), classroom assessment and research (Cross and Steadman 1996), and the scholarship of teaching and learning (Huber and Morreale 2002). Each of these faculty development practices conforms to those ideas.

Values. We could make the same argument around the issue of values. Values are internal to the learner, but they are derived from and responsive to the environment. Developers can structure activities that are built upon the values of the faculty member. Those activities that best reflect the faculty member's preexisting values are more likely to be undertaken willingly.

A good example of using values is the rise of interest in incorporating service learning into courses. Faculty who value their ability to support the community would be encouraged to think about ways of making that support visible and part of the values that they teach. In 2001, leading researchers from this area published a report on the use of service learning in college students, faculty, institutions, and communities (Eyler et al. 2001). The overall findings were very encouraging to those who wanted students to become more engaged in the community at many levels. Programs like the ones reported could be initiated as a way of giving faculty who have civic engagement as a core value an opportunity to develop their own interest further while also inculcating those same values in their students.

Expectancies. Placed in the external factors line with curiosity and values in the MVP model, expectancies are most likely pointing toward the faculty member's beliefs about his own skills and ability to be successful in a given area. Once again, these self-beliefs include the feeling of efficacy. However, we could also suggest that those expectations for success come from interactions with the environment in terms of prior success with similar activities in other contexts. This is the most likely interpretation we should give the wording of the MVP model. A problem with this interpretation is that the most relevant expectations of most faculty revolve around the institution's expectations. Bess (1998) believes that the base structure of tenure follows the professional path structure more readily than a hierarchical structure of outside control. He asserts, "The standards of professional behavior, inculcated during education and training, are presumed to be firmly implanted as intrinsic standards. Further, the commonality of those standards allows peer systems of professionals to agree when there is apparent deviance" (1998, 8). So, we expect a faculty member to uphold the standards of the discipline and the academy in general within the university context. The faculty member's own role expectations may add some other constraints on behavior. Development programs must align with those internal and external expectations if they are to be helpful to the faculty member.

For example, a female faculty member at a major research university might be held up to graduate students as an example of a successful academic and a model that the students should emulate. That position places many restrictions on what she should and should not do. A faculty developer at her institution will need to be aware of the pressure to conform to the expectations under which the faculty member is working. The developer can create mentorship opportunities linking her to more senior female faculty to discuss the impact of those expectations—others' as well as her own—on her work and her personal life. Other faculty development activities surrounding the expectations component might be regular programs that bring faculty and administrators together to discuss expectations of the institution or efforts to develop clearer guidelines for faculty that mesh the institution's values with those of the faculty.

As the model shows, "inputs" combine and lead to "outputs." The presence of faculty development activities might influence curiosity at the Psychological environment level and initial "Effort direction" in MVP Segment 1. It could also connect to and influence interest in participating in programs designed to track tendencies of faculty in the same position, leading to opportunities for collaborative efforts.

MVP Segment 2. Even when effort direction has been pointed toward a worthwhile and exciting goal, the faculty member has to begin to turn direction into action. This is the "Effort initiation" component in MVP Segment 2. This does not happen automatically, especially in the face of competing goals of equal value. Developers have often been thwarted by the experience of having a faculty member become excited about a new instructional model and decide to implement it the next semester, only to have the enthusiasm wane over any short delay between the faculty colloquium and the time for course planning. As with any new behavior, the earliest implementation steps are the hardest and therefore most likely to slip away like disappearing New Year's resolutions.

This is the challenge of the second step in implementation: commitment. Creating a psychological environment that supports commitment to implement the new behavior is critical. This would preferably be a public commitment along with an initial action step. For example, to promote the effort initiation process, many development sessions now end with having faculty fill out a plan of action in writing while they are still at the motivating event and then discuss it with other faculty who are also intending to implement the behavior change. Organizers sometimes designate these other faculty as "collaborators" or "supporters" and suggest that pairs of faculty schedule a time in the near future to check in with one another to maintain their motivation through peer pressure. This can serve as part of the positive commitment intentions in the psychological environment category.

A related implementation influence is represented by the advent of faculty learning communities (Cox 2001). Often referred to as FLCs, these small groups of faculty interested in the same new methodology will work together over a longer period of time but are especially helpful in getting group members over those initial trials. Similar in nature to the collaborators or supporters mentioned previously, these learning communities provide ongoing support and engage in scholarly study of the innovation they are attempting. They also cross over into the volitional influences category that are discussed next. This is the MVP Segment 3 output, "Effort persistence."

Another influence in implementation is more negatively felt by new users. This is a fear of failure or a lack of self-confidence about trying something new. This influence is related to several other motivation theories such as self-efficacy (Bandura 2001) or goal orientation theory (Grant and Dweck 2003; Elliot and Church 1997; Elliot, Murayama, and Pekrun 2011), each of which revolves around the positive and negative affect and behavior involved in trying something new.

Here is a real-world example of overcoming initial failure concerns. Recognizing that the initial implementation is often a stumbling block, support needs to be in evidence and readily accessible to the faculty member during the early stages of an activity. This has been a major problem in encouraging faculty to use new technology in many classes. Because most new technology seems a total "black box" to new users, they experience great concern that what looks so easy in a demonstration will fail miserably in front of a class. In some institutions, several support systems have been tried. Many faculty development programs employ a small cadre of tech-savvy students, who are assigned to a faculty member for at least the first weeks of class to be present in case something goes wrong. Once the instructors get control of the equipment, they are usually willing to be weaned from having an outside person in the class and will continue on their own.

MVP Segment 3. Volitional influences are part of supporting the initial steps in implementation and will frequently convince an instructor to at least try a new strategy. However, this does not guarantee continuation. Even the most well-intentioned individual can have difficulty sticking to a plan in the face of other equally important goals or a continued high level of effort required to maintain the innovation over time. The ability of an individual to adhere to a new program requires volitional strategies centered around effort persistence. These are actions that an individual can use to keep going in the face of obstacles. For example, in the case of a newly developed intention to use technology, an instructor might create action checklists for each class period to make sure that she is able to follow the sequence correctly without missing any steps. As she becomes more proficient, this checklist can be pared down to just a few important cues.

Volition also requires monitoring the environment to catch changes that might signal the need for a new strategy. For example, an instructor might include activities to check whether students understand main ideas. A common example is the "think–pair–share" process, which involves teaming students and then having them summarize what they think they understood. The teacher then takes a class poll about that understanding before proceeding. Student response systems ("clickers") or "smartphone" technologies can streamline this process and provide tabulated results.

Volition involves a faculty member being alert to his own well-being so that he can maintain a level of calm in the face of frustrating obstacles. It might be as simple as pausing when something goes wrong to take a deep breath and engage in some calming self-talk before acting. All of these actions are under the control of the instructor so that he can optimize his performance through self-regulation and have the resources and ability to persist even when things are not going well.

Faculty development centers recognize that they cannot be available every time faculty need their support. As a result, they try to build ways for instructors to get answers to their questions just in time. One of the earliest attempts to meet this need was done at the University of California Berkeley by Robert Wilson, a pioneer in faculty development (Wilson 1987). The practice of student evaluations of teaching was just beginning, and, to make the ratings more useful to skeptical faculty, Wilson recruited some recipients of institutional teaching awards to explain their most successful teaching practices as identified by high ratings on items from their students. Their "best practices" descriptions were synthesized and tied to the appropriate student ratings items. In future semesters, when an instructor received student ratings results, she also received a personalized "Berkeley Personal Teaching Guide," consisting of her end-of-semester student ratings and best practices descriptions for the four items that students had rated as NOT representative of her teaching. The hope was that instructors could use the descriptions to inspire changes in their own practices. This served to remind faculty of practices to consider: a sort of indirect guide to self-regulation that appeared regularly. More recent technological supports make it possible for these links to successful practices to always be available online. Instructors puzzling over what to do about a less than satisfactory result either from student ratings or about any implementation of a new teaching method can consult these best practices sites for ideas or answers to their questions. This can have the unintended, but desirable effect of empowering faculty to seek their own answers in the vast literature on teaching that is becoming readily available and searchable, thus enhancing their self-regulating actions. However, as Michael Theall notes in Chapter 7 of this issue, if evaluation is poorly done, the results can have undesirable effects on motivation and can reduce teachers' Effort initiation and Effort persistence in Segments 2 and 3 of the MVP model. Because a primary purpose of professional development programs is to promote faculty engagement in exploration and improvement of teaching and learning, it seems clear that programs for development and evaluation should have related purposes and should be structured and carried out in ways that maximize support for teaching and learning. These programs and their productive outcomes must be institutionally protected, and top-level administrative actions should make this support clear and public.

MVP Segment 4. The process of self-regulation for effort persistence is closely tied to the external inputs influencing motivation and volition. In fact, Segment 4 is really describing the kinds of things that are required during self-regulation in Segment 3, especially when there are threats to volition. The kinds of actions that are basic to self-regulation are the monitoring and management activities that are the mark of metacognition. Metacognition is defined as the process of monitoring one's thinking and control processing. The primary difference between metacognition and the total concept of self-regulation is that metacognition is the control of the cognitive aspects of self-regulation. These involve maintaining focus and engagement, being aware of the planning and execution of the targeted action, and monitoring what is going right and what is going wrong. The processes go on in the background rather than being the actions themselves. For that reason, it is difficult to teach these processes, so most programs to enhance metacognition focus on just the types of external behavior that might indicate that metacognition is occurring. These include activities like planning and setting goals, creating pro and con charts to help in making decisions, gathering and analyzing data about outcomes, and, especially, reflecting on what is happening or has happened. This last action is the first action of MVP Segment 6, observing and evaluating consequences and experiencing the satisfaction or frustration of positive versus negative outcomes. Although we always experience consequences of any action we take, it is rare that, in the heat of the moment, we stop to reflect on what has happened and what might have caused that outcome. If, as faculty developers, we want faculty to learn from their teaching experiences, we need to foster this reflection in them and in ourselves. Here are two examples from practice of maximizing the impact of metacognition and reflection.

Example 1. This example involves individual consultation. In this faculty development practice, when a faculty developer consults with an instructor directly, much time is spent conducting the process in a manner that matches the MVP model. So, for example, most consultations begin with an understanding of why the faculty member is requesting assistance, of both internal influences and external influences, of what her desired outcomes of acting would be, and how they would be measured. This gives direction to the effort. Once a plan of action has been determined, most consultations include a type of behavior "contract" that specifies what is going to be done by both the consultant and the instructor. The contract usually includes a timetable that can be consulted later as a way of measuring fidelity of implementation of the plan or of determining what needs to be changed. This plan serves to spur effort initiation and sets up the monitoring that is important later in the implementation and self-regulation components of the sequence.

The consultant works with the faculty member closely during the early stages of implementation, but gradually shifts from being a direct presence to an "as needed" consultant, hoping that the instructor can self-regulate now that things are moving along. This would be similar to the persistence efforts that an individual might do alone, and it involves metacognitive monitoring that is part of mental resource management.

Midway through the semester, the two meet for a "how is it going" assessment and to review the initial plan and outcome measures to determine if the program needs adjusting to respond to new challenges. Although this is done in a meeting between the consultant and the faculty member, the faculty member has previously been asked to reflect in writing on a few questions about the implementation that will be discussed during that meeting. The consultant and instructor discuss ways of maintaining progress that has been made, consider new strategies, and possibly create documents that can be used for summative evaluation by others in the teaching review part of promotion and tenure. This basic format for implementing an MVP process can be done individually by the faculty member in the format of a reflective log that includes the initial analysis, the plan, regular reflections in a journal and a summative evaluation to be filed with a portfolio for external evaluation documents.

Example 2. Perhaps the implementation that is truest to the MVP model is a faculty learning community. Actually very similar to the Harvard Assessment project noted in this chapter, the FLC idea began in the early 2000s as an outgrowth of peer learning theory and research in educational psychology. It spread rapidly into higher education teaching and faculty development practice (Cox 2001). The reasons for the popularity of FLCs can be found in the degree to which they, more than any other faculty development practice, illustrate the tenets of the MVP model.

Learning communities exemplify some of the most strongly held values of higher education—faculty ownership and academic freedom. The communities are built around faculty interests and values and organized and run by faculty themselves, thus giving them a lot of stake in their success. They bring together faculty with like minds who are making a public commitment to their peers to pursue a joint project over a course of weeks or months rather than in a single afternoon's workshop. They generally have regular meetings, which serve to keep their commitment to the project strong. They share interesting insights into the joint project topic that is focused rather than diffuse. They are actively engaged in conducting their own learning process and generally very motivated by seeing other faculty who serve as role models for deep involvement. They are in "learning" communities, and so they will be learning new skills and ideas and looking for evidence of learning not just for themselves, but to share with other members of the community. Their discussions are opportunities for reflection and emotional support. And on virtually every campus at which they have been tried, they have the support of the administration.

If I were asked for a good example of faculty development based on motivation as drawn by Keller's model, I can't think of a single one that would surpass the faculty learning community.

References

Bandura, Albert. 2001. "Social Cognitive Theory: An Agentic Perspective." *Annual Review of Psychology* 52: 1–26.

Bess, James. 1977. "The Motivation to Teach." *Journal of Higher Education* 48(3): 243–258.

Bess, James. 1997. "The Motivation to Teach: Perennial Conundrums." In *Teaching Well and Liking It*, edited by James Bess, 424–439. Baltimore: Johns Hopkins University Press.

Bess, James. 1998. "Contract Systems, Bureaucracies, and Faculty Motivation: The Probable Effects of a No-Tenure Policy." *Journal of Higher Education* 69(1): 1–22.

Blackburn, Robert T., Jeffery P. Bieber, Janet H. Lawrence, and Lois Trautvette. 1991. "Faculty at Work: Focus on Research, Scholarship and Service." *Research in Higher Education* 32: 385–413.

Blackburn, Robert T., Janet H. Lawrence, Jeffery P. Bieber, and Lois Trautvette. 1991. "Faculty at Work: Focus on Teaching." *Research in Higher Education* 32: 363–383.

Cox, Milton. 2001. "Faculty Learning Communities: Change Agents for Transforming Institutions into Learning Organizations." *To Improve the Academy. Vol.* 19, edited by Devorah Lieberman and Catherine Wehlburg, 69–93. Bolton, MA: Anker Publishing.

Cross, K. Patricia, and Mimi H. Steadman. 1996. *Classroom Research: Implementing the Scholarship of Teaching*. San Francisco: Jossey-Bass.

Deci, Edward L., and Richard M. Ryan. 2000. "The 'What' and 'Why' of Goal Pursuits: Human Needs and the Self-Determination of Behavior." *Psychological Inquiry* 11: 227–268.

Elliot, Andrew J., and Marcy A. Church. 1997. "A Hierarchical Model of Approach and Avoidance Achievement Motivation." *Journal of Personality and Social Psychology* 72(1): 218–232.

Elliot, Andrew J., Kou Murayama, and Reinhard Pekrun. 2011. "A 3×2 Achievement Goal Model." *Journal of Educational Psychology* 103(3): 632–648.

Eyler, Janet, Dwight E. Giles, Christine M. Stenson, and Charlene J. Gray. 2001. *At a Glance: What We Know about the Effects of Service-learning on College Students, Faculty, Institutions, and Communities, 1993–2000*. Nashville, TN: Vanderbilt University.

Fenstermacher, Gary, and Virginia Richardson. 1994. "Promoting Confusion in Educational Psychology: How Is It Done?" *Educational Psychology* 29(1): 49–55.

Grant, Heidi, and Carol S. Dweck. 2003. "Clarifying Achievement Goals and Their Impact." *Journal of Personality and Social Psychology* 85(3): 541–553.

Huber, Mary, and Sherwin P. Morreale. 2002. "Situating the Scholarship of Teaching and Learning: A Cross-Disciplinary Conversation." In *Disciplinary Styles in the Scholarship of Teaching and Learning: Exploring Common Ground*, edited by Mary Huber and Sherwin P. Morreale, 1–43. Washington, DC: American Association for Higher Education and the Carnegie Foundation for the Advancement of Teaching.

Keller, John. 2010. "An Integrative Theory of Motivation, Volition, and Performance.' *Technology, Instruction, Cognition and Learning* 6(2): 79–104.

Light, Richard. 1990. *The Harvard Assessment Seminars: Explorations with Students and Faculty about Teaching, Learning, and Student Life. First Report*. Cambridge, MA: Harvard University Graduate School of Education.

Richlin, Laurie, and Milton Cox, eds. 2004. *Building Faculty Learning Communities*. New Directions for Teaching and Learning, no. 97. San Francisco: Jossey-Bass.

Ryan, Richard M., and Edward L. Deci. 2000. "Self-Determination Theory and the Facilitation of Intrinsic Motivation." *American Psychologist* 55(2): 68–78.

Wilson, Robert. 1987. "Toward Excellence in Teaching." In *Techniques for Evaluating and Improving Instruction*. New Directions for Teaching and Learning, no. 80, edited by Lawrence M. Aleamoni, 9–24. San Francisco: Jossey-Bass.

MARILLA D. SVINICKI is professor of psychology at the University of Texas at Austin.

7

This chapter considers faculty evaluation and motivational and volitional issues. The focus is on the ways in which faculty evaluation influences not only faculty attitudes and beliefs but also willingness to engage in professional development and instructional improvement programs. Recommendations for effective practice that enhances motivation are included.

MVP and Faculty Evaluation

Michael Theall

In Chapter 6 of this issue, Marilla Svinicki discussed the relationships of the motivation–volition–performance (MVP) model to faculty and professional development. This chapter deals with another topic that is equally important because of its potential impact on faculty motivation and volition: faculty evaluation. Faculty evaluation and development cannot be considered separately. The reason for this link can be succinctly put: evaluation without development is punitive, and development without evaluation is guesswork. There is a parallel here to effective assessment because that involves more than giving a learner a test and grade. It includes a review of the strengths and weakness in performance, relating those findings to student characteristics, to content level and difficulty, and to the design and delivery of instruction. Effective assessment provides learners with suggestions or strategies for capitalizing on strengths and overcoming weaknesses. Faculty evaluation coupled with development must do the same. When the only result of evaluation is a negative review, motivation, volitional action, and performance can be diminished, and when evaluation is done poorly, individual reputations and careers can be damaged, teaching and learning suffer, and student attrition can increase. There are good reasons for concern.

Complaints about Faculty Evaluation

One obvious example of evaluation without development is seen when data—especially student ratings of teaching—are improperly collected, reported, and interpreted and thus misused. Over several decades, no issue in higher education teaching and learning has given rise to more research, more opinion, and more complaints, resistance, and hostility. Aside from the innately threatening nature of evaluation, there are good reasons for the ongoing conflict about ratings. Three major problems relate to this situation. First, ratings are often the only kind of data used. This is a methodological and administrative mistake. Second, ratings are incorrectly constructed, poorly administered, and/or improperly analyzed and reported. These are psychometric and operational problems. Third, ratings results are often misunderstood, misinterpreted, and misused. These are problems caused by lack of knowledge. Finally, ratings are often mistakenly referred to as student evaluations of teaching or SETs. This is a semantic error and a problem because students are not the evaluators. They are providers of one kind of data. The true evaluators are the faculty and administrators who make judgments. But when ratings questionnaires use value-loaded items asking students to express likes or dislikes or to give opinions about what is good or bad, or when items ask for opinions students are unqualified to give (rating teacher knowledge is the most common and egregious example), then ratings take on a different and more objectionable nature.

However, the purpose of this section is not to restate the long student ratings debate. Evidence of the reliability and validity of ratings and their potential usefulness abounds, and strategies for good faculty evaluation practice have been presented over the last four decades (Arreola 2007; Benton and Cashin 2012; Berk 2006; Centra 1993; Doyle 1975; Theall 2010a; Theall and Franklin 1990). The recommendations in this literature are consistent and can be simply stated: (1) completely describe the nature and extent of the work expected and the criteria associated with specific levels of performance; (2) use multiple sources of data from all concerned stakeholders related to all expected areas of performance; (3) with student ratings, use validated, psychometrically sound instruments; (4) analyze and report results in accurate and understandable ways to faculty members and to those who will make evaluative decisions; and (5) provide training for those involved so that collection, interpretation, and use of results are accurate and decisions are equitable. The more important discussion in this issue is about the relationships of faculty evaluation to motivation and volition and about improving evaluation practice to enhance faculty desire and will to take deliberate, positive, and if necessary, corrective action.

MVP and Evaluation

Two characteristics of the model are important to this discussion.

The MVP Model Is Dynamic. In the model, "External inputs" interact with and influence "Psychological environments" in all six segments, but the interactions are not necessarily sequential. Interactions or events anywhere in the model can influence other parts of the model. A simple example would be a situation in which stress about evaluation could influence mental resource management activities in Segment 4, thus affecting performance in Segment 5, with consequences in Segment 6 that could greatly affect motivation and expectancies identified in Segment 1. For purposes of this description, we can consider faculty evaluation and the related processes of promotion and tenure to be common sources of considerable stress for faculty. Anticipation of being evaluated could cause anxiety and lead to elevated effort in Segments 1, 2, and 3. Effort is usually a positive thing, but under stressful circumstances that effort may be disorganized and excessive, creating cognitive and emotional overload that could negatively affect information processing, mental management, and performance. If the outcome is not a desired one, disappointment and emotional reactions can result in defensiveness, reduction of confidence, lowered self-concept, more negative expectancies, a more external locus of control, and unproductive attributions about the causes of the evaluation results. This kind of negative outcome leads us to a second characteristic of MVP.

The MVP Model Is Cyclical. Even though the model is dynamic, it also has a cyclical nature that can lead in either positive or negative directions. The intent, of course, is that sound motivational design and practice will lead to a productive cycle in which learners follow an effort–process–performance–satisfaction path and that the satisfaction will support continuation of this sequence. The same applies to faculty evaluation. However, poor evaluation practice can have a reverse effect, and when support resources are not available, satisfaction, motivation, volition, and performance are diminished. This sequence can lead to more serious problems like those discussed by David Machell (1989). He used the title "professorial melancholia" (PM) for professional emotional dysfunction in a three-stage process and said that it could be related to the peculiarities of the professor's role. He defined PM as, "a progressive emotional process characterized by the negating of a university professor's professional motivation, positive attitudinal focus, and personal esteem" (Machell 1989, 41). In the Early Stage, discouragement and frustration can be accompanied by beginning resentment of students and administration, self-fortification, and withdrawal. The Middle Stage includes increases in these negative feelings as well as disillusionment, depression, and anger. In the Late Stage, students and administrators become enemies, behavior becomes more aggressive, and extreme cases can involve rage, verbal abuse of students, possible drug and alcohol abuse, and burnout. The MVP model explains professorial melancholia from a different perspective, but the parallels are striking. Even when motivation, volition, expectancies, and effort are high (as in the excitement of beginning a new faculty position), the pressures of contemporary faculty roles and responsibilities can quickly take their toll. When, as is often the case with new teachers, student ratings are not strongly positive (a frequent event given that new faculty are often assigned to teach large-enrollment, out-of-major, entry-level courses where teaching is more difficult and ratings have been shown to be lower on average), it is no wonder that frustration with ratings and students can arise. As Todd Zakrajsek points out in Chapter 2 of this issue, there is evidence that emotions, anxieties, and negative expectancies can be shared among groups through the process of social contagion. This can happen among faculty with respect to evaluation, and when ratings are misused, faculty can begin to frame a narrative that is defensive and includes negative external attributions. This "narrative emplotment" (Hladkyj et al. 1999), can open Machell's (1989) Stage One and the negativity becomes more defensive and dangerous as time goes on. When the direction of MVP is unproductive, conclusions reached in Segment 6 strongly and negatively influence motivation and volition in Segments 1, 2, and 3, as well as effective activity and performance in Segments 4 and 5. Ultimately, faculty may retreat from teaching and all forms of professional development. Faculty cannot teach effectively if they hold negative views about students, peers, or administrators or negative expectations about their performance and course outcomes.

How Can Good Evaluation Practice Enhance Motivation, Volition, and Performance?

Good evaluation practice can alleviate many common problems. The use of a poorly constructed student ratings instrument is a frequent problem, but well-researched and validated instruments are available. Instruments and process used in peer and administrator evaluation can also be problematic, but open discussion and public agreement on process can help to avoid these difficulties. Misunderstanding about and misinterpretation and misuse of ratings and other data can lead to disputes and resistance (Franklin and Theall 1989), but training for those who provide and use data can lessen the impact of such errors. Having development resources directly associated with the evaluation process is always necessary, but development can never be presented as prescriptive or only for those who might experience problems. The notion of a "clinic for sick teachers" is not only unacceptable because of its poor choice of words, it is destructive in its impact on motivation and volition. Evaluation should provide data that engage, enhance, and enliven dialogue about teaching and learning. For example, a good evaluation system can be used to identify excellence in teaching and can be supplemented by establishing programs in which excellent teachers share their experience and insights with others. That same system should be able to isolate specific conditions like class size or subject matter that affect teaching and learning so that discussions can be more focused and precise. As well, that system should be able to establish norms and criteria associated with those specific conditions so that comparisons can be fairly made. A common error in evaluation has been to compare individuals without considering the contexts in which they are teaching. For example, comparing the mean overall rating of a new teacher in a 200-student, introductory mathematics course to that of an experienced teacher in a 15-person graduate seminar—even in the same discipline—violates the most basic rules of psychometrics, reasonable decision making, and fair practice. Thus, a good evaluation system should be able to provide decision makers with sound bases for using available data, and the system should be regularly updated and statistically revalidated to establish new norms and determine whether criteria for comparisons should be changed. The best examples of this need are found in recent changes in student demographics and in course delivery. Comparing a traditional teaching situation to an online situation may not be legitimate even in the same subject at the same level with the same teacher and class size. Comparing two teachers in these situations is more prone to error, especially if the teachers themselves have different amounts of training on the use of the technologies.

Recognizing the Cultures and Differences across the Academy

Another important aspect of productive evaluation is that it is sensitive to local context and culture. Bergquist and Pawlak (2008) discussed the variety of differences across "the six cultures of the academy," noting that the differences were significant enough to be considered in many aspects of administration and institutional policy. Feldman and Paulsen (1999) wrote about the role of a "supportive teaching culture" that had six elements including connecting rigorous evaluation of teaching to promotion and tenure decision making. Similarly, a "supportive evaluation culture" would include careful review of performance expectations and the criteria to be used in assessing that performance, dialogue and shared decision making about evaluation instrumentation and process, clear and public guidelines about the data to be used and the rules for fairly interpreting those data, and equity in assignment of rewards. Theall and Arreola (2006) proposed that college teaching was a "metaprofession": a profession that required multiple sets of skills beyond content expertise. They identified twenty skill sets and developed a matrix that displayed the skill sets and the frequency of need for those skill sets in four roles: teaching, scholarship, service, and administration. Their later research reported by Theall (2010b) revealed that faculty in different disciplines had significantly different opinions about the importance of the skill sets in each of the roles, and they also had different opinions when self-reporting their own expertise in the skill sets. As well, faculty and administrators showed significant differences of opinions about the importance of the skill sets. Opinions were also different across different Carnegie types of institutions. The conclusion drawn from this work was that there is no one set of evaluation criteria that can be imposed on all institutions, colleges, departments, or disciplines. Importantly, if administrative decision makers value skill sets differently than the faculty they are evaluating, then evaluative decisions can be biased. Further evidence of differences that can affect evaluation comes from Diamond and Adam's work on faculty rewards (1995, 2000). They found wide-ranging opinions about the value of various kinds of scholarly, professional, and creative work. Disciplinary differences have been well established in the evaluation of teaching. Cashin (1990) reported significantly different average overall ratings across disciplines. Analyses of other major evaluation data show the same result. Franklin and Theall (1992) explored these differences by investigating instructional strategies across disciplines. They found that disciplines with the highest average ratings employed instructional objectives at the higher end of the taxonomy of objectives (Bloom et al. 1956) whereas the lowest rated disciplines used objectives at the lower end of the taxonomy. Highly rated disciplines also employed active learning strategies as opposed to lecturing, and these disciplines used varied assessment methods rather than relying on one or two major in-class tests. Finally, with specific respect to motivational issues, Wlodkowski and Ginsberg (1995) discussed "a motivational framework for culturally responsive teaching." They argued that effective instruction must include consideration of the diversity among students and the differences in motivation that this diversity can incorporate. Their framework had four elements focused on inclusion, attitude, relevance, and competence. This framework applies to faculty evaluation as well. Without faculty partnership in decisions about all aspect of the evaluation process, there will be suspicions about fairness and equity. This will not enhance motivation and confidence. Indeed, it may well result in motivation to subvert the system or to seek evidence supporting claims that the system is invalid and unreliable. The long history of small-scale studies intended to "prove" that student ratings are invalid attests to this defensive posture. The use of a "top-down," imposed system will reduce opportunities for productive use of evaluation data and without a companion system for professional development, there will be little confidence in the process and less incentive to engage in development activities. From a cultural perspective, poor evaluation practice violates many of the values and traditions dear to the faculty. Resistance to such systems is not only understandable, it is justified.

What Is a Good Evaluation System Like?

A good evaluation system must be able to explore such issues in order to provide the most valid and reliable data and to establish guidelines for valid and reliable decision making. Good evaluation practice should incorporate all six segments of the MVP model. Though evaluation results often appear after the fact of teaching—that is, as Consequences affecting Satisfaction in Segment 6—the cyclical nature of the model immediately connects these consequences to the Psychological environment in Segments 1, 2, and 3, with a potentially powerful affect and equally strong effect on motivation and volition. Good evaluation should provide understandable results and strategies for interpreting and using these results in ways that are positive and productive: even if they indicate weak performance. If this is done, there will be reasons for the teacher to accept the results and use them for purposes of improvement. The actions can include development activities, working with peers, trying new teaching methods, carefully collecting and using assessment data, and monitoring progress. The MVP model works in faculty development and evaluation just as it does with teaching and learning: as a process and pathway that can bring teaching and learning—teachers and learners—closer to each other and to success.

References

Arreola, Raoul A. 2007. *Developing a Comprehensive Faculty Evaluation System*, 3rd ed. San Francisco: Jossey Bass.

Benton, Steven L., and William E. Cashin. 2012. *Student Ratings of Teaching: A Summary of Research and Literature*. IDEA Paper no. 50. Manhattan, KS: IDEA Center. http://www.ideaedu.org/Portals/0/Uploads/Documents/IDEA%20Papers/IDEA%20Papers/PaperIDEA_50.pdf

Bergquist, William H., and Kenneth Pawlak. 2008. *Engaging the Six Cultures of the Academy: Revised and Expanded Edition of the Four Cultures of the Academy*. San Francisco: Jossey Bass.

Berk, Ronald A. 2006. *Thirteen Strategies to Measure College Teaching*. Sterling, VA: Stylus Publishing.

Bloom, Benjamin S., Max D. Englehart, Edward J. Furst, Walker H. Hill, and David R. Krathwohl. 1956. *Taxonomy of Educational Objectives. The Classification of Educational Goals. Handbook I: Cognitive Domain*. New York: David McKay.

Cashin, William E. 1990. "Students Do Rate Different Academic Fields Differently." In *Student Ratings of Instruction: Issues for Improving Practice*. New Directions for Teaching and Learning, no. 43, edited by Michael Theall and Jennifer L. Franklin, 113–121. San Francisco: Jossey Bass.

Centra, John A. 1993. *Reflective Faculty Evaluation: Enhancing Teaching and Determining Faculty Effectiveness*. San Francisco: Jossey-Bass.

Diamond, Robert M., and Bronwyn E. Adam. 1995. *The Disciplines Speak. Rewarding the Scholarly, Professional, and Creative Work of Faculty*. Washington, DC: American Association for Higher Education.

Diamond, Robert M., and Bronwyn E. Adam. 2000. *The Disciplines Speak II. More Statements on Rewarding the Scholarly, Professional, and Creative Work of Faculty*. Washington, DC: American Association for Higher Education.

Doyle, Kenneth O. 1975. *Student Evaluation of Instruction*. Lexington, MA: D. C. Heath.

Feldman, Kenneth A., and Michael B. Paulsen. 1999. "Faculty Motivation: The Role of a Supportive Teaching Culture." In *Motivation from Within: Approaches for Encouraging Faculty and Students to Excel*. New Directions for Teaching and Learning, no. 78, edited by Michael Theall, 69–78. San Francisco: Jossey Bass.

Franklin, Jennifer L., and Michael Theall. 1989, March 31. "Who Reads Ratings: Knowledge, Attitudes, and Practices of Users of Student Ratings of Instruction." Paper presented at the 70th annual meeting of the American Educational Research Association. San Francisco. ERIC ED306241.

Franklin, Jennifer L., and Michael Theall. 1992, April 22. "Disciplinary Differences, Instructional Goals and Activities, Measures of Student Performance, and Student Ratings of Instruction." Paper presented at the 73rd annual meeting of the American Educational Research Association. San Francisco. ERIC ED346786.

Hladkyj, Steve, Jason R. Taylor, Sarah T. Pelletier, and Raymond P. Perry. 1999, April 21. "Narrative Emplotment: Meaning and Value in Unpredictable Experience and its Role in Student Motivation." Paper presented at the 80th annual meeting of the American Educational Research Association. Montreal, Canada.

Machell, David F. 1989. "A Discourse on Professorial Melancholia." *Community Review* 9(1–2): 41–50.

Theall, Michael. 2010a. "Evaluating Teaching: From Reliability to Accountability." In *Landmark Issues in Teaching and Learning. A Look Back at New Directions for Teaching and Learning*. New Directions for Teaching and Learning, no. 123, edited by Marilla. D. Svinicki and Catherine M. Wehlburg, 85–95. San Francisco: Jossey Bass.

Theall, Michael. 2010b, June 28. "Opinions of Faculty and Academic Administrators about the Roles, Work, and Skills of the Professoriate: A Model for Organizational Development." Presentation at the annual meeting of the International Consortium for Educational Development. Barcelona, Spain.

Theall, Michael, and Raoul A. Arreola. 2006. "The 'Meta-Profession' of College Teaching." *Thriving in Academe* 22(5): 1–5.

Theall, Michael, and Jennifer L. Franklin, eds. 1990. *Student Ratings of Instruction: Issues for Improving Practice*. New Directions for Teaching and Learning, no. 43. San Francisco: Jossey Bass.

Wlodkowski, Raymond J., and Margery E. Ginsberg. 1995. *Diversity and Motivation: Culturally Responsive Teaching*. San Francisco: Jossey Bass.

MICHAEL THEALL is emeritus professor of education, Youngstown State University.

8

This chapter applies John Keller's MVP model and, specifically, adapts the ARCS-V components of that model—defined and described in Chapter 1 of this issue of New Directions for Teaching and Learning*—as a frame for exploring practical, research-based assessment, and feedback strategies and tools teachers can use to help students enhance, manage, and sustain their own motivation to learn.*

Assessing Motivation to Improve Learning: Practical Applications of Keller's MVP Model and ARCS-V Design Process

Thomas A. Angelo

Efforts to enhance student motivation to learn in higher education often focus on how faculty can promote and enhance motivation by changing teaching strategies or course designs. This chapter focuses, instead, on using assessment and feedback as levers to help students understand, enhance, and sustain their own motivation to learn. To those ends, the chapter offers teachers' practical guidelines and research-based assessment, and feedback strategies and tools they can adapt and apply in a range of courses and disciplines to help students become more self-motivating, self-regulating, and independent learners. It makes use of, and slightly adapts, John Keller's motivation–volition–performance (MVP) model and, specifically, the attention, relevance, confidence, satisfaction, volition (ARCS-V) components of that model (2010)—defined and described in Chapter 1 of this issue of *New Directions for Teaching and Learning*—as a framework for organizing and implementing these assessment, self-assessment, and feedback strategies and tools.

The intended purpose of the strategies and tools presented is twofold. First, they can provide teachers with information needed to focus, monitor, and improve the effectiveness of their efforts to enhance student motivation. At the same time, and more important, they can provide students with ways to self-assess, enhance, self-regulate, and maintain their own motivation to learn long after final exams have ended and beyond graduation. Given the length limitations of this chapter, it is not possible to include detailed

New Directions for Teaching and Learning, no. 152, Winter 2017 © 2017 Wiley Periodicals, Inc.
Published online in Wiley Online Library (wileyonlinelibrary.com) • DOI: 10.1002/tl.20272

descriptions of these strategies and tools. Readers will, instead, be directed to relevant resources online and in print.

Five Practical Guidelines for Assessing Motivation to Improve Learning

The following five guidelines, based on the author's experience, may prove useful to consider even before selecting specific assessment strategies and tools. First, Make Your Own Implicit Assumptions and Biases Explicit. When teachers talk about student motivation to learn, it can sound like stereotyping. We bemoan the burden of dealing with students who are unmotivated to learn and talk longingly of the pleasures of teaching the self-motivated. Listening to such conversations, one could get the impression that students are either motivated or not; that motivation to learn is a fixed and immutable outcome of nature or nurture or both.

To anyone who has closely observed students, however, this "fixed" view of motivation must seem highly unrealistic. As any parent can attest, almost all young people willingly devote large amounts of time and energy to learning about or how to do particular things. The objects of their passionate interests are, of course, not always those that parents and teachers might prefer. Even the most highly academically motivated learner is unlikely to be equally interested and invested in every course. Thus, the very same student who seems, and perhaps is, totally unmotivated to learn in my required course may be the keenest, most dedicated scholar in my colleague's elective. It is, therefore, salutary for teachers to remind ourselves that we typically see only a very small sample of our students' lives from which it is unfair and unwise to generalize. If we choose to assess only students' interest in the specific topics we teach, we need to be aware that we risk mistaking one tree for the forest. Making our implicit assumptions explicit to ourselves and others can help us determine whether and how to assess student motivation and inform analyses of the results.

Second, Recognize That Students Are Not Unbiased Self-Reporters. Although no one knows more about their motivation to learn than the students themselves, their self-reports, like all self-reports, are likely be biased. Haddon and McKay (2015, 19) note that "social desirability bias" and "reference bias" are common problems. Social desirability bias occurs when learners represent their motivations as more positive than they really are in order to "look good" to themselves and others. For example, students may tell teachers what they think we want to hear, especially if they suspect their responses are not anonymous. Reference bias exists when learners' standards for self-assessing motivation are influenced by those around them. Surround yourself with highly motivated, disciplined peers and you may report your own level of motivation lower than you would if your reference group were all low-achieving "slackers." In addition, reported motivation can be temporarily influenced by immediate circumstances, such as earning a very high or very low grade on an important test or assignment.

These and other biases inherent in self-reporting can be mitigated by carefully selecting or constructing assessment instruments and questions, by ensuring anonymity, by taking multiple soundings over time, and by judicious interpretation of responses. Consequently, although students' self-reports can provide teachers with information useful for understanding and improving learning motivation, that same self-report information is not sufficiently accurate or reliable to be used to make important decisions on matters such as admissions or grades or to assess program, course, or teaching effectiveness.

Third, Do No Harm. Suppose teachers assess students' motivation to learn in their courses at the start of term. Suppose further that the majority of students report they are not at all motivated to learn those subjects. It seems quite possible that such findings might demotivate those teachers, causing them to lower their expectations or even to become cynical about their students. At the same time, if those assessment results were shared with students, such information might further lower their motivation to learn. Lack of enthusiasm can, after all, be just as contagious as enthusiasm. Not sharing the infelicitous assessment results would pose risks, as well, since students would likely draw their own conclusions from silence. Consequently, it is important to weigh carefully the potential risks and benefits of assessing learner motivation before asking the first question.

Fourth, Don't Assess Unless You Are Prepared to Respond to All Likely Outcomes. One simple approach to risk mitigation is to ask, prior to doing any assessment: "If the results of my assessment were X or Y or Z, what could I do with that information to enhance students' motivation to learn?" Result X might be the hypothetical scenario presented previously: Most or all students report they are unmotivated. Result Y might indicate that the class is split between those who are and those who are not. Result Z might be that almost all the students were highly motivated to learn the material. Each potential result would require very different responses. Sketching a plan in advance for predicting likely obstacles and devising strategies for overcoming them can improve the likelihood of a positive outcome for teachers and learners alike (Oettingen 2014).

Fifth, Remember That Motivation to Learn Is Alterable and That You Can Influence It. However bad the news, even if it's Result X, the good news is that motivation to learn is contextual, variable and, consequently, also alterable. To enhance learner motivation most effectively, teachers need specific information that only their students can provide. To that end, we need focused assessment strategies and tools. In addition, teachers also need strategies and tools for providing useful feedback. Students, for their part, need teacher feedback, of course, but they also need self-assessment tools to help them become more aware of and better able to monitor, enhance, and maintain their own motivation to learn. The remainder of this chapter aims to provide both students and teachers with more leverage to raise and sustain motivation.

The Proposed M-ARCS-V Model of Motivation

In Chapter 1 of this issue, Keller explains the MVP model of motivation and ARCS-V applications to instructional design. As a reminder, the letters in the ARCS-V acronym stand for attention, relevance, confidence, satisfaction, and volition. Building on that chapter, I propose adding one more category to Keller's model. Then I apply the slightly revised model as a framework for assessing and providing feedback on student motivation to learn.

Research by Dweck (2006, 2012) and others (Burnette et al. 2013) provides strong evidence that motivation to learn is largely dependent on students' academic mind-sets—their implicit beliefs about their own intelligence and capacity to learn. Convinced of the power of these implicit self-theories, and of the usefulness of Keller's model, I propose adding mind-set as the initial category, thereby creating the M-ARCS-V model of learning motivation. In the remainder of this brief chapter, I offer suggestions on assessing and giving feedback related to each of the six categories of the M-ARCS-V model.

Mind-Set

Simply put, "academic mind-set" consists of the usually implicit belief system that a person has regarding intelligence, ability, and formal learning. Learners with "growth" or "adaptive" mind-sets believe that, with the appropriate effort and support, they can learn, achieve, and succeed—effectively becoming more intelligent (Dweck 2012). As Schroder and others (2014) explain: "Decades of research suggest that mindsets substantially influence learning, motivation and achievement . . . . A consistent finding is that a belief in the malleability of self-attributes – a growth mindset – is associated with better performance and perseverance, especially when individuals are faced with challenging tasks" (2014, 27).

Learners with a "fixed mind-set," on the contrary, believe that intelligence is largely if not totally inherited or innate and unchangeable. As Paulsen and Feldman (1999) reported, years before the term "mind-set" became popular, "Students with the naïve belief that the ability to learn is fixed were less likely to have an intrinsic goal orientation, to appreciate the value of learning tasks, to perceive an internal control over learning, and to feel efficacious about their ability to learn" (21). Consequently, students with fixed mind-sets are less likely to respond to teachers' efforts to enhance motivation to learn. Hence, my argument for beginning with "M" for mind-set.

Assessing Mind-Set. Free online tools for self-assessing mind-set can be found at Carol Dweck's website (www.mindsetonline.com) and at

Stanford University's Project for Education Research that Scales (PERTS) website (www.perts.net). The Mindset Meter on the PERTS website can provide teachers with a summary of students' mind-set survey results. Both websites also provide information on mind-set research, links to references, and practical advice for teachers.

Feedback on Mind-Set. The good news is that fixed academic mind-sets can be changed. To that end, PERTS has focused on developing, field testing, and researching "mind-set interventions"—"psychologically powerful activities designed to change the way students think about learning and school in targeted ways." Recent experimental research, with both school and college students, has demonstrated that relatively brief and simple online mind-set interventions —typically short readings and reflective writing exercises—can result in significant improvements in conceptual learning and grades. For an in-depth treatment and college-level examples from several disciplines, see Chapter 6, "Mindset Matters," in Saundra McGuire's *Teach Students How to Learn* (McGuire, 2015, 60–71).

Attention

In Chapter 1, Keller identifies the "attention" category in ARCS-V with arousal and interest. This section focuses on the interest aspect. Research has repeatedly shown that when learners feel intrinsic interest in a topic—that is, interest generated from within, independent of external rewards or punishments such as praise and grades—they are more likely to be motivated to learn deeply and well and to persevere in their learning.

Assessing Interest. One simple formative approach to assessing students' interest in course topics is to administer a brief inventory: a list of course topics and/or subtopics, each followed by response options (Angelo and Cross 1993). For example, in assessing my students prior to the first class meeting, I ask them to indicate their level of interest in each course topic using the following scale: 0 = No interest in the topic; 1 = Interested only in an overview; 2 = Interested in reading about and discussing; 3 = Interested in learning how to apply this; 4 = Interested in doing in-depth research for my paper/project. Students may also nominate other course-related topics in which they are personally interested.

Feedback on Interest. Students benefit both from receiving a copy of their interest inventory self-assessment responses and from seeing the aggregate responses of the class. Typically, there is a range of interest in most topics but also a handful of topics of high interest to most students. I share inventory results with students to illustrate the diversity in their interests and to explain why some topics get more emphasis than others. Whenever possible, I also begin courses with a high-interest topic or two and inform students I am doing so in response to their feedback. Finally, I encourage students whose interests are not included in the syllabus to consider pursuing their topics through research papers or projects.

Relevance

In this context, "relevance" refers to students' perceptions that the learning outcomes and requirements of a course or program are consistent with and will contribute to the realization of their aspirations and goals. Thus, students might find a particular required course relatively uninteresting but still see it as relevant to achieving their goals and, therefore, be motivated to learn the course material well. We might predict that, on average, the greater the perceived congruence between individual learner goals and course goals, the higher the level of intrinsic motivation. In the following example, I focus on assessing and giving feedback on students' learning goals as a way to enhance perceptions of relevance.

Assessing Learning Goals. Simply Google "goal-setting tools online free" and you will find a number of options. But how effective are these free tools? Morisano and others (2010) provide evidence that a rigorously research-based, but relatively simple and inexpensive eight-step intervention focused on goal setting and elaborating and commitment can improve student academic motivation and performance.

Feedback on Learning Goals. One way to enhance students' perceptions of the relevance of courses is to provide feedback on the degree to which their learning and academic goals overlap with course learning outcomes. For example, once students have set their goals using the Morisano et al. (2010) intervention, feedback can be provided to individuals and groups of students regarding the degree of overlap. An even simpler technique, known as Goal Ranking and Matching (Angelo and Cross 1993), was designed to provide just such "overlap" feedback to teachers and students.

Confidence

In Chapter 1, Keller says, "Confidence in ARCS-V . . . refers to the positive expectancies for success, experiences of success, and attributions of successes to one's own abilities." One critical aspect of this cluster is academic self-efficacy, defined as the learner's perception of his or her ability to successfully complete a specific task or achieve a specific goal—specific being the operative word. I may lack confidence in my ability to succeed as a biology major, for example, but feel high self-efficacy regarding my competence in identifying the birds found in my area, or vice-versa. High self-efficacy tends to correlate with high motivation to learn specific topics and skills.

Assessing Self-Efficacy. Albert Bandura, who defined and developed the concept of self-efficacy, helpfully provided us with a "Guide for Constructing Self-Efficacy Scales" (2006). Bandura's chapter contains examples and guidelines that can easily be adapted to any task or topic. An excellent example of a Bandura-inspired scale created by faculty for a specific discipline, and of published research done with that instrument, can be found

Table 8.1. Exam/Assignment Wrapper

Pre-Questions	*Post-Questions*
1. What is the minimum grade you would be satisfied to earn?	1. What is the actual grade you earned? How satisfied are you with that grade?
2. How are you specifically planning to earn that grade? (For example: How and how much will you study?)	2. What did you do, specifically, to earn that grade?
3. Of things you can control, what might prevent you from earning that grade?	3. If you didn't earn the grade you hoped to, what prevented you from doing so? [If you did, how specifically did you do so?]
4. What specifically will you do to avoid that?	4. If you didn't earn the grade you hoped to, what might you do differently next time to achieve a more satisfactory outcome? [If you did, what might you apply in future to succeed again?]

in Finney and Schraw's (2003) article on assessing student self-efficacy in college statistics.

Feedback on Self-Efficacy. As noted early in this chapter, students are not always accurate assessors of their own knowledge, skills or, in this case, self-efficacy. Nonetheless, assessing students' perceived self-efficacy about specific aspects of a course can provide teachers with valuable information on which tasks or topics students might be most motivated to tackle first. As Keller notes in Chapter 1, identifying gaps between students' perceptions and their actual performance can be used to motivate, if the feedback and follow-up are handled effectively.

Satisfaction

According to Keller (Chapter 1), "Satisfaction, ... refers to positive feelings about accomplishments and learning experiences, feelings which are key to sustaining one's motivation to learn."

Assessing Satisfaction. There are, of course, many ways to assess student satisfaction with learning experiences, including via questions included in evaluation of course and teaching forms. Such feedback, however, typically comes too late to be formative and is focused entirely on teacher behaviors, encouraging a student-as-consumer mind-set. One promising tool for promoting formative student self-assessment of satisfaction is a simple pre- and postsurvey known as a "cognitive wrapper" or "exam/assignment wrapper." An example of the latter is provided in Table 8.1. See Lovett (2013) and Winkelmes (2013) for research on exam wrappers and Jose Bowen's website (www.teachingnaked.com) for examples of more general cognitive wrappers.

Feedback on Satisfaction. This approach emphasizes helping students take responsibility for their own satisfaction, which contributes to self-management, justified self-efficacy, and confidence. To those ends, feedback on satisfaction should focus on helping students develop high but realistic expectations regarding academic success, as well as the self-regulation and study strategies needed to achieve that success.

Volition

Volition is undoubtedly the least familiar term in the ARCS-V model; it refers to the everyday concepts of willpower and perseverance: The ability to strive over time and overcome challenges to achieve an important goal. Recently, the old-fashioned term "grit" has come to be a synonym for volition, and the role of grit in academic and life success has received a great deal of attention from researchers, educators, journalists, employers, and the general public. Angela Duckworth is credited with developing and publicizing grit, which she defines as "perseverance and passion for long-term goals," noting that grit "entails the capacity to sustain both effort and interest in projects that take months or even longer to complete" (Duckworth and Quinn 2009, 166). If mind-set is the cornerstone for improving motivation to learn, then grit is the capstone.

Assessing Grit

The Duckworth Lab website (https://sites.sas.upenn.edu/duckworth) offers free access to a "12-Item Grit Scale" and other related instruments useful to students and teachers alike, as well as research reports and journal articles.

Feedback on Grit. The online "Grit Scale" can provide students with a simple "grittiness score" in an instant. Providing useful feedback to those who rate low on "grittiness," however, is a much more complicated task and much less researched than the concept of grit or its measurement. Research indicates that grittiness is positively correlated with having a higher "purpose for learning"—learning goals motivated by connections beyond one's own self-interest (Yeager et al. 2014). Thus, it would appear that helping students discover and elaborate their intrinsic goals and make connections to "self-transcendent" goals may enhance perseverance. Second, grittiness is also related to effective self-regulation and self-management skills. To that end, we can provide students with feedback on and instruction in those metacognitive skills. Specifically, we can help students learn how to engage in deliberate practice—disciplined approaches to study and learning that lead to persistence and mastery (Duckworth et al. 2011).

A Final Note

Keller's ARCS-V and MVP models provide a useful framework for organizing assessment and feedback to enhance motivation to learn. If we take a systems view, then each category of the ARCS-V model represents a leverage point at which teachers and students can collaborate to assess/self-assess, diagnose, provide feedback and, as needed, intervene to raise the overall level of learning motivation and, consequently, of academic achievement and success. This chapter argues that integrating the research-based concepts of "academic mind-set" and "grit" into the ARCS-V model could further enhance its explanatory power and practical usefulness.

References

Angelo, Thomas A., and K. Patricia Cross. 1993. *Classroom Assessment Techniques: A Handbook for College Teachers*, 2nd ed. San Francisco: Jossey-Bass.

Bandura, Albert. 2006. "Guide for Constructing Self-Efficacy Scales." In *Self-Efficacy Beliefs of Adolescents*, edited by Frank Pajares and Tim Urdan, 307–337. Charlotte, NC: Information Age Publishing.

Burnette, Jeni L., Ernest H. O'Boyle, Eric M. VanEpps, Jeffrey M. Pollack, and Eli J. Finkel. 2013. "Mindsets Matter: A Meta-Analytic Review of Implicit Theories and Self-Regulation." *Psychological Bulletin* 139: 655–701.

Duckworth, Angela Lee, and Patrick D. Quinn. 2009. "Development and Validation of the Short Grit Scale (Grit-S)." *Journal of Personality Assessment* 91(2): 166–174.

Duckworth, Angela Lee, Teri A. Kirby, Eli Tsukayama, Heather Berstein, and K. Anders Ericsson. 2011. "Deliberate Practice Spells Success: Why Grittier Competitors Triumph at the National Spelling Bee." *Social Psychological and Personality Science* 2(2): 174–181.

Dweck, Carol S. 2006. *Mindset: The New Psychology of Success*. New York: Random House.

Dweck, Carol S. 2012. "Mindsets and Human Nature: Promoting Change in the Middle East, the Schoolyard, the Racial Divide, and Willpower." *American Psychologist* 67(8): 614–622.

Finney, Sara J., and Gregory Schraw. 2003. "Self-Efficacy Beliefs in College Statistics Courses." *Contemporary Educational Psychology* 28: 161–186.

Haddon, Susan, and Sarah McKay. 2015. *Motivation Matters: How New Research Can Help Teachers Boost Student Engagement*. Stanford, CA: Carnegie Foundation for the Advancement of Teaching.

Keller, John M. 2010. *Motivational Design for Learning and Performance*. New York: Springer.

Lovett, Marsha C. 2013. "Make Exams Worth More than Grades: Using Exam Wrappers to Promote Metacognition." In *Using Reflection and Metacognition to Improve Student Learning*, edited by Matthew Kaplan, Naomi Silver, Danielle Lavaque-Manty, and Deborah Meizlish. Sterling, VA: Stylus.

McGuire, Saundra. 2015. *Teach Students How to Learn: Strategies You Can Incorporate into Any Course to Improve Student Metacognition, Study Skills, and Motivation*. Sterling, VA: Stylus.

Morisano, Dominique, Jacob B. Hirsh, Jordan B. Peterson, Robert O. Pihl, and Bruce M. Shore. 2010. "Setting, Elaborating, and Reflecting on Personal Goals Improves Academic Performance.' *Journal of Applied Psychology* 95(2): 255–264.

Oettingen, Gabrielle. 2014. *Rethinking Positive Thinking: Inside the New Science of Motivation*. New York: Penguin.

Paulsen, Michael B., and Kenneth A. Feldman. 1999. "Student Motivation and Epistemological Beliefs." In *Motivation from Within: Approaches for Encouraging Faculty and Students to Excel*. New Directions for Teaching and Learning, no. 78, edited by Michael Theall, 17–25. San Francisco: Jossey-Bass.

Schroder, Hans S., Tim P. Moran, M. Brent Donnellan and Jason Moser. 2014. "Mindset Induction Effects on Cognitive Control: A Neurobehavioral Investigation." *Biological Psychology* 103: 27–37.

Winkelmes, MaryAnn. 2013. "Transparency in Teaching: Faculty Share Data and Improve Students' Learning." *Liberal Education* 99(2): 48–55.

Yeager, David S., Marlone D. Henderson, David Paunesku, Gregory M. Walton, Sidney D'Mello, Brian J. Spitzer, and Angela Lee Duckworth. 2014. "Boring But Important: A Self-Transcendent Purpose for Learning Fosters Academic Self-regulation." *Journal of Personality and Social Psychology* 107(4): 559–580.

THOMAS A. ANGELO is clinical professor in the UNC Eshelman School of Pharmacy at the University of North Carolina at Chapel Hill.

9

This brief chapter outlines themes and ideas drawn from this issue.

Summary and Recommendations

Michael Theall, John M. Keller

Integrating and applying models is not a simple task in teaching and learning contexts. As the chapters in this issue have shown, the range of factors that can affect teaching and learning is wide and the number of variables involved is very large. Even with respect to a focused topic such as motivation, it is neither practical nor reasonable to assume that any one model will apply to all situations or even that it will work in the same way across similar situations. Thus, although this issue presents examples of integration and application, it does not propose that the motivation–volition–performance (MVP) model is the answer to all motivational questions. Nor do we suggest that its use will guarantee that teachers can successfully identify the individual, contextual, disciplinary, or psychological differences that exist in the teaching and learning processes or create instruction that will suit every set of conditions. However, what we do offer is a carefully developed framework supported by literature from a wide range of disciplines. This framework is useful for considering motivational issues and when appropriate, designing instruction that takes into account many of the factors that allow learners to find interesting directions to follow, to develop and initiate plans for exploring new ideas, and to develop habits of thought and action that persist over time and promote academic and personal achievement. Because the MVP model is cyclical, it reinforces the need for useful feedback that allows meaningful review of events and reasonable interpretation of the consequences of behavior. This feedback is powerful because it demonstrates the need to carry out purposeful action in order to achieve goals, and when outcomes are positive, it provides intrinsic reinforcement for persisting in productive habits. When learners are introduced to constructs such as locus of control, self-regulation, and attribution theory, the value of the model becomes more apparent: it not only guides the design of instruction, but even if outcomes are not completely positive, it allows learners to better understand the important relationships between effort and performance.

New Directions for Teaching and Learning, no. 152, Winter 2017 © 2017 Wiley Periodicals, Inc.
Published online in Wiley Online Library (wileyonlinelibrary.com) • DOI: 10.1002/tl.20273

Ideas for MVP Segments 1, 2, and 3

The following paragraphs outline some of the major themes and ideas drawn from this issue's chapters.

Structure. Teachers can provide syllabi, process guides, concept maps, timelines, and other resources that help learners to see the organization in a course or a subject and also help learners to get themselves more organized in response to course requirements. Clear structure should not be confused with rigid adherence to a set of rules, but rather should be a framework within which the motivational and volitional requirements are understood. Providing a solid structural foundation allows learners to better understand their responsibilities and to more carefully plan their effort. Given that "teaching students to think like a professional ________" is important in so many disciplines, discussing the epistemology of the discipline and how and why the course teaches disciplinary habits of thought and action that prepare students for professional life is critical to understanding the structure and to establishing the relevance of the course and its content and process.

Goals, Requirements, and Expectations. For both teachers and learners, successful performance requires full and precise description of goals, requirements, performance criteria, and constraints. Goals can be imposed (as in assignments) or self-determined (as in long-range planning), but in either case, goal setting is the first step in establishing reasons for planning, initiating, and persisting in willful action. When goals are further defined in terms of their sequence and relationships (as in reaching a short-term goal in order to be able to proceed to a longer term goal), they provide both direction and organization.

Expectancies. Teachers and learners must believe that their efforts will result in desired outcomes. This is not always the case, and therefore, it is important to demonstrate that goals can be reached through planning, action, and ongoing monitoring of performance. It is not sufficient to simply state that effort results in a perfect outcome every time. Expectancies must be tied to an understanding of students' past performance, abilities, and resources as well as to the demands of the content and the discipline.

Ideas for MVP Segments 4 and 5

Motivational design is not a strictly linear process.

Flexibility and Creativity. Mental resource management and the mental activities of learning differ across individuals. Allowing teachers and learners to experiment with new ideas and to examine alternatives increases relevance and the degree of independence they need to initiate action. Independence also fosters internal locus of control and even if experiments do not always work out successfully, valuable learning can take place.

Opportunities for Elaboration of Ideas. A powerful way to promote "deep approaches" to learning and the development of affective outcomes such as values, commitment, and professional behavior is to engage learners in identifying and considering their own value systems and attitudes. Motivationally, this increases relevance and it also promotes metacognitive activity as students not only learn about course content but about the discipline and about themselves. Synthesis and creativity require this kind of cognition strategies that include elaboration support improved engagement and memory function for learning.

Notice-to-Expert Pathways. For learners, long-term goals may seem vague, but one way to provide a focus is to demonstrate the connections of course process and content to those distant goals. This increases the relevance of class work and also increases the expectancy of reaching goals. Incremental achievement—possible with carefully designed, progressively complex tasks and frequent formative assessment—supports motivation and positive expectancies. Modeling professional habits of thought and action also points toward successful long-term outcomes.

Community and Collegiality. Much has been written about collaborative teaching and learning and about the value of working with peers. Whether in collaborative projects, problem-based activities, or faculty learning communities, the benefits of having the support of group members and sharing ideas have been consistently demonstrated.

Ideas for MVP Segment 6

Motivational design, like any systematic design process, requires rigor.

Assessment and Evaluation. Instructional systems design requires careful consideration of both enabling and terminal outcomes; thus, systems for formative and summative assessment should target specific behavioral and other indicators of achievement, employ sophisticated psychometric procedures, use efficient data collection and management systems, and provide meaningful analysis with reporting formats that are easily understood and interpreted. Faculty and students often need assistance in using assessment and evaluation data, especially with respect to satisfaction and attributional issues.

Conclusions

The ARCS-V model was developed independently of these other approaches but they are compatible with it.

Integrity of the Models. A primary goal of the attention, relevance, confidence, satisfaction, volition (ARCS-V) model is to synthesize associated concepts based on shared attributes and thus to provide a parsimonious foundation for research and application. However, it is commonplace in the psychological literature for an idea to be introduced that is a variation of existing concepts or theories even though it may contain a new metaphor or perspective. Such is the case with "mind-set" (Dweck 2006) and "grit" (Duckworth and Quinn 2009), which were proposed by Thomas Angelo in Chapter 9 and which offer us an excellent opportunity to provide further explanation of key aspects of the ARCS-V and MVP models. Both mind-set and grit are important but fall within the range of concepts contained in the Confidence and Volition segments of the models (Keller 2010). Thus, it would add redundancy to these models to add these concepts as new categories. However, any variable within the model can be highlighted as being particularly important in a given situation. These models are system models with systematic processes and interactions among all of their components, which means that if an analysis reveals problems with the mind-set of the audience, that can be a starting point for intervention. Angelo's suggestions for assessing these concepts and other concepts in the models are most welcome because many teachers might have difficulty developing ways to explore them and to make effective instructional adjustments.

Cyclical Nature of the Model. In closing, the cyclical nature of MVP must be kept in mind. Just as a positive outcome can enhance motivation and volition, an incorrectly interpreted negative outcome can reduce motivation and volitional effort. If we want to enhance motivation and achievement, we think of MVP as a dynamic system whose process can be altered by contextual changes at any time. Fortunately, the MVP framework can be used as a guide for adapting to change and helping others to focus their energy, effort, and action on achieving important goals.

The cyclical nature of MVP must be kept in mind as well. Just as a positive outcome can enhance motivation and volition, an incorrectly interpreted negative outcome can reduce motivation and volitional effort. If we want to enhance motivation and achievement, we must be mindful of this potential and think of MVP not as a rigid system but rather a dynamic one whose process can be altered by contextual changes at any time. Fortunately, the MVP framework can be used as a guide for adapting to change and helping others to focus their energy, effort, and action on achieving important goals.

References

Duckworth, Angela L., and Patrick, D. Quinn. 2009. "Development and Validation of the Short Grit Scale (Grit-S)." *Journal of Personality Assessment* 91(2): 166–174.

Dweck, Carol S. 2006. *Mindset: The New Psychology of Success*. New York: Random House Publishing Company.

Keller, John M. 2010. *Motivational Design for Learning and Performance: The ARCS Model Approach*. New York: Springer.

MICHAEL THEALL is emeritus professor of education, Youngstown State University.

JOHN M. KELLER is professor emeritus of the Department of Educational Psychology and Learning Systems, Florida State University.

INDEX

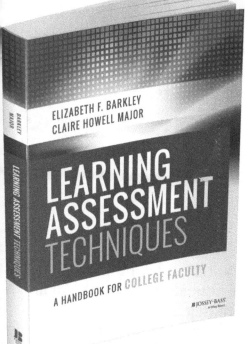